T0286060

Upcycling Furniture & Home Decor

by Judy Rom

Champion of Upcycling at UpcycleThat.com

A Wiley Brand

Upcycling Furniture & Home Decor For Dummies®

Published by: **John Wiley & Sons, Inc.,** 111 River Street, Hoboken, NJ 07030-5774, www.wiley.com

Copyright © 2023 by John Wiley & Sons, Inc., Hoboken, New Jersey

Published simultaneously in Canada

For general information on our other products and services, please contact our Customer Care Department within the U.S. at 877-762-2974, outside the U.S. at 317-572-3993, or fax 317-572-4002. For technical support, please visit https://hub.wiley.com/community/support/dummies.

Wiley publishes in a variety of print and electronic formats and by print-on-demand. Some material included with standard print versions of this book may not be included in e-books or in print-on-demand. If this book refers to media such as a CD or DVD that is not included in the version you purchased, you may download this material at http://booksupport.wiley.com. For more information about Wiley products, visit www.wiley.com.

Library of Congress Control Number: 2023933138

ISBN: 978-1-394-15002-1 (pbk); ISBN 978-1-394-15004-5 (ebk); ISBN 978-1-394-15003-8 (ebk)

SKY10047784_051223

Contents at a Glance

Table of Contents

Introduction

Welcome to *Upcycling Furniture & Home Decor For Dummies*! If you're reading this book, you must be interested in upcycling. Upcycling is taking something that's considered waste, and turning it into something more functional, beautiful, and valuable. Congratulations for being savvy! Upcycling is truly the best way to get stylish and original furniture and home decor. It's fun, good for the environment, affordable, and oh so satisfying!

This book is for aspiring fixer-uppers. If you've never done it before, upcycling may seem daunting. But don't fret; this book will be your guide. I'll show you step by step how to source and transform items to give them a new lease on life.

About This Book

Have you ever seen amazing upcycled pieces and wondered how they were created? This book illuminates the process and sets you up with everything you need to know to start. *Upcycling Furniture & Home Decor For Dummies* makes upcycling projects easy and enjoyable.

In no time at all you'll be updating items with your own unique flair and even selling your pieces if you want to. Because upcycling should be fun and accessible, this book is divided into six piece-of-cake parts:

>> **Part 1, "Getting Started with Upcycling":** Explore what upcycling is and find out how to save items from the landfill. Experience the thrill of the hunt! Here I explain where to find items, and how to increase their value with your ingenuity.

>> **Part 2, "The Big Upcycle: Preparing and Painting Your Piece":** Gain clarity on how to prepare your piece so that it lasts. I walk you through the tools of the trade and explain the techniques of priming, painting, and sealing. This section covers lots of amazing expertise for enhancing patina (rustic charm and aging), as well as how to add the finishing touches to take your pieces to the next level.

>> **Part 3, "Other Upcycling Techniques":** Find out easy and specific ways to upcycle. Discover the revitalizing techniques of reupholstery; delve into the world of glass-cutting; and get pro tips for sourcing and reusing reclaimed wood.

>> **Part 4, "Upcycling Tutorials for Your Home":** Pick up the processes for upcycling furniture like desks, tables, chairs, and more. Work through tutorials one step at a time to learn how to reimagine furniture and home decor.

>> **Part 5, "The Four Ps of Selling Your Pieces":** After you've had some practice, you may want to reap the rewards of selling your creations. The four Ps — props, photography, pricing, and promotion — are key to lining up customers. I share how to style, stage, and photograph your items. I also take the guess-work out of pricing and promotion, so that you can confidently sell with sizzle.

>> **Part 6, "The Part of Tens":** Certain items are always great for upcycling. Find out what they are so that you can nab 'em when you see 'em. It's ideal to reuse items that you naturally have a lot of, like glass mason jars. Get wise to the top ten ways to repurpose them.

Foolish Assumptions

This book is for people who want to turn trash into treasure. It's for anyone who's curious about learning how to upcycle furniture and home decor. Maybe you want to create upcycled items for your home or as a fun hobby that you can make money doing. I've assumed that you've probably never done an upcycling project before, but that you're thrifty and eco-conscious.

Perhaps you already have some items that you'd like to refresh, but you're not sure how to start. Even if you're not naturally crafty, this book shows you how to transform and repurpose with panache.

Icons Used in This Book

Throughout this book, icons in the margins call out for your attention. These icons highlight certain types of valuable information. Here are the icons that I use, with a brief description of each one.

The Tip icon marks practical tips and shortcuts you can use to make upcycling easier.

REMEMBER

Remember icons mark the information that is especially important to know. They help you to avoid common pitfalls. When you see this icon, you know that the information is important enough to read twice.

WARNING

The Warning icon tells you to watch out. It marks important information that could be detrimental to your success while upcycling. This icon isn't used a lot, so pay attention when you see it.

Beyond the Book

In addition to the abundance of information and guidance related to upcycling that I provide in this book, you get access to even more help and information online at `https://dummies.com`. Check out this book's online Cheat Sheet for information about where to find materials and what to look out for. To find it, go to `https://dummies.com` and search for "Upcycling Furniture & Home Decor For Dummies Cheat Sheet."

You can find even more upcycling information and inspiration on my website, `www.upcyclethat.com`.

Where to Go from Here

How you read this book is totally up to you. Start from the top to get excited about upcycling and to discover where to find inspiration and materials.

The linear route sets you up with the foundational knowledge of how to prepare for upcycling and brings you up to date on upcycling techniques you can use. Or, you might be raring to go and prefer to drop right into specific tutorials. Each chapter stands on its own, so feel free to reference chapters as you see fit.

Regardless of whether you go front to back or pick and choose, this book is ready to launch your adventures in upcycling. Let's get started!

1
Getting Started with Upcycling

Dive into the world of upcycling with inspiring examples of "trash" turned into treasure.

Find out how you can create value and income while also saving furniture from going to the landfill.

Discover which materials are best for upcycling and where to find them. Gain crystal-clear clarity on what to look for when you're sourcing.

Learn how to use mood boards, color schemes, and sketches to activate your creative juju and bring your unique designs to life.

Chapter **1**

Getting Excited about Upcycling

There are a myriad of reasons to get excited about upcycling. To begin with, upcycling is like modern-day alchemy. It transforms unwanted items into highly prized pieces. It's like turning trash into treasure!

Another reason to get into upcycling is that it's eco-conscious. In a world experiencing a garbage crisis, upcycling is a part of the solution. It feels positively magnificent to rescue and reimagine items headed for the landfill. Also, it's downright thrilling selling pieces for a profit. That's right — upcycling is an environmentally-savvy hobby that can earn you cash.

In this chapter, I explain what upcycling is and explore its benefits. You'll also discover the first steps of upcycling and find the inspiration you need to start. Prepare to see the world around you differently!

Upcycling Explained

Upcycling is taking something that otherwise would be considered waste and reusing it. Often the item is reimagined with an entirely different purpose.

TIP

It's called *upcycling* because the value of the item increases. It becomes more functional and beautiful than what it previously was.

Understanding the difference between upcycling and recycling

Upcycling and recycling aren't the same because they have different processes. With recycling, items are broken down before they're reused. For example, plastic is shredded and melted down into pellets.

As the material is recycled, its value degrades, so the process of recycling is sometimes referred to as downcycling. For instance, recycled plastic isn't as valuable as virgin plastic, and can only be recycled a finite number of times.

Whereas downcycling reduces the value of an item, upcycling increases it. The item is reimagined and reborn. It goes from being an unwanted discard to a highly sought-after and valued piece. It's an inspiring journey!

Discovering the benefits of upcycling

The benefits to upcycling are plentiful but include environmental, creative, and financial. Here are some of the top advantages:

>> **Upcycling is good for the environment:** First and foremost, upcycling is great because it reduces the waste that ends up in a landfill. Beyond that, as items are reused, the demand decreases for raw materials to create new products. This in turn lowers air and water pollution. It's like a snowball effect for environmental conservation.

>> **Upcycling encourages creativity:** Upcycling ignites your creativity. It's an innovative process with no limits. Plus, getting crafty and doing it yourself is satisfying.

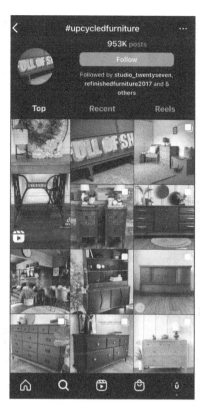
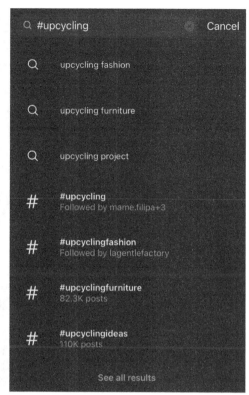

FIGURE 3-3:
You can search via hashtag on Instagram (left), and check out the related hashtags is an effective way to find new content (right).

To save a post, tap and hold the tag icon and select or create the collection you want to save it to. Figure 3-4 shows how to do it.

To see your saved collections on the Instagram app, use the following steps:

1. **Go to your profile by clicking on your profile picture at the bottom right.**
2. **Tap on the three horizontal lines at the top right.**
3. **Click the tag that says Saved.**
4. **Either select All Posts or click a collection to see your saved posts.**

The right side of Figure 3-4 shows how the collections feature looks.

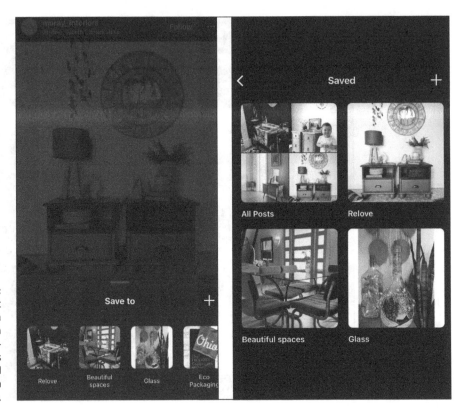

FIGURE 3-4:
Saving a post
to a collection
on Instagram
(left) and revis-
iting the posts
you've saved
on Instagram
(right).

Another way to save photos from Instagram is to take screenshots and save them to your camera roll. To do this on an iPhone, quickly press and release the side (formerly called the power button) and the volume buttons at the same time. On an Android, simultaneously press the volume and power buttons.

TIP

Making Mood Boards

Mood boards are a fabulous way to kickstart the creative design process. They allow you to visualize and organize your ideas and emotions. A mood board helps you define the style and overall look of your project.

Mood boards can be composed of a mix of photographs or screenshots that you've taken; pictures from magazines; colors, textures, and reference projects you like; or really anything that inspires you. Mood boards can be physical or digital.

>> **Upcycling saves money:** Upcycling furniture instead of buying it new can save you thousands of dollars. It's also an attainable way to get custom, one-of-a-kind pieces.

>> **Upcycling generates value and income:** Upcycling and reselling furniture and home decor is an awesome side hustle. It's a smart way to make money by being creative.

>> **Upcycling is beautiful:** Upcycled items are often bespoke. These items feature custom artisanship and are stylishly unique.

>> **Upcycling is fun and accessible:** Anyone can be an upcycler. With a bit of passion and commitment, you too can learn how. The materials are just waiting to be discovered, and finding them is one of the best parts.

>> **Upcycling is inspiring:** The flash of inspiration to upcycle can come from the most unexpected pieces. That's part of the magic. Once you start creating, you won't want to stop.

>> **Upcycling is meaningful:** Upcycled pieces have a history and character to them that you just don't find with "fast furniture" (low-quality, mass-produced furniture that's being rapidly bought, used briefly, and quickly discarded). The item has already lived a life (or two), and that makes it special. In addition, upcycling supports local artisans.

Entering the World of Upcycling

You begin upcycling either by using what you already have, or by scouring for materials with a project in mind.

Starting with materials in hand

When you already have the materials, there's a great opportunity to use your imagination. Do you want to repaint and refinish the item, or do you want to repurpose it into something completely new?

TIP

Think about what the item *could* become. Figure 1-1 On the left is a door that was converted into a table. On the right is an epic coffee table made from a dresser drawer. Find out how to make it in Chapter 12.

FIGURE 1-1:
Door table by
Curtis Smeltzer
of Handy
Father LLC
(left). This
gorgeous
coffee table by
Judy Rom was
made from a
dresser drawer
found in an
alley (right).

Working toward an end-use vision

Alternatively, you might have a piece of furniture or decor that you want to create, like a dramatic light fixture, and just need to find the supplies. You can repurpose glass plates and bowls into light shades, like in Figure 1-2.

TIP

Charming glassware is waiting to be rescued at your local thrift shop.

Upcycling Inspiration for Your Home

Upcycling is your opportunity to get creative. You can upcycle furniture in thousands of ways. In this section, I provide lots of visual inspiration!

Fun, yet functional furniture

Sometimes it takes removing part of the original item to repurpose it. On the left of Figure 1-3 there's an awesome bathroom vanity made from a dresser. Charlotte Smith of At Charlotte's House refinished this piece and used a jig to cut out a place for the bathroom sink and faucet. She also retrofitted the drawers so they'd still be functional. To finish the piece, the artisan applied a heavy-duty sealant to the dresser to keep it from warping in the humidity of the bathroom.

Sometimes the piece needs to be added to. On the right of Figure 1-3, there's an IKEA cabinet that Teofi González of The Kiyomi transformed by adding a veneer cutout and gorgeous pastel hues. Trendy new legs complete the look.

FIGURE 1-3:
Bathroom
vanity by
Charlotte
Smith (left).
Reimagined
cabinet by
Teofi González
(right).

The console on the left of Figure 1-4 appears perfectly worn and weathered. This stunning coastal look was achieved by painting it with multiple colors and layers, using salt wash for texture and then sanding it smooth. On the right of Figure 1-4, you see a curvy, scalloped dresser that was completely transformed with a white, turquoise, teal, and deep blue ombre. The upcycler perfectly accented the piece with gold leaf to create a stunning geode design.

Eye-catching home decor

Home decor is important because it sets the tone for your home. Style is completely subjective, and you can express yourself in unlimited ways.

FIGURE 1-4:
Weathered
console table
by Michelle
Dickson and
Stephanie
Hofer of Sunny
Side Design
(left). Geode
cabinet by Kate
Anderson of KT
Designs (right).

Vinyl records will always have that cool factor. Unfortunately, they're often scratched beyond use. Turning them into home decor is a great way to keep the music alive. The top left of Figure 1-5 shows a record turned into a bowl.

The skateboard decks–turned–shelves shown in the bottom left of Figure 1-5 are ideal for a skater.

Denim upcycles are classic. You can turn ripped jeans into multiple creative home furnishings, like those shown in the top right and bottom right in Figure 1-5.

Lamps that light the way

Upcycled lighting will really brighten up your life. There are lots of inventive ways to reimagine items into lights. Repurposing an item as a lamp shade for a pendant light is one of the most effective ways to create a light source.

TIP

You can buy a pendant light cord from your local hardware store or online.

At the top of Figure 1-6, Heinz Beanz cans have been turned into funky pendant lights by Willem Heeffer, a Dutch designer.

It's also possible to make lamps out of electrical wire, light sockets, and a lamp switch wire and plug. The phone lamp in the middle left of Figure 1-6 was DIY-ed by Judy Rom and Bart Taylor with those items, a bit of imagination, and an old rotary phone.

A Sputnik-style light on the middle right of Figure 1-6 is a modern take on upcycled lighting. Sputnik lamps have multiple arms that each have a bulb. This kind of fixture became popular in the Atomic Age (1940–1960s) when the first satellite orbited Earth. This stunning Sputnik chandelier with Depression glass used as shades was designed by Jeff Risinger and Mark Winn of BootsNGus.com.

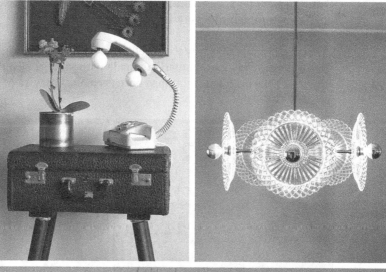

FIGURE 1-6: Iconic cans turned into pop art lighting (top). Retro phone reimagined (middle left). Upcycled plates are illuminated by this gorgeous Sputnik chandelier from Jeff Risinger and Mark Winn of BootsNGus.com (middle right). Rainbow mason jar chandelier from Jeff Risinger and Mark Winn of BootsNGus.com (bottom).

Multiple items look gorgeous grouped together as a chandelier. The bottom of Figure 1-6 features a stunning rainbow chandelier by Jeff Risinger and Mark Winn of BootsNGus.com made with painted mason jars. The center ring used here is made from solid wood. Additionally, the lids have been drilled to allow heat to escape so that the jars won't overheat.

Gorgeous garden upcycles

You won't believe the extent of what you can upcycle into planters. The top left of Figure 1-7 shows an incredible TV-turned terrarium.

Covering plant pots with a burlap coffee bean bag is a delightful way to dress them up! The bottom left of Figure 1-7 shows the look.

Upcycling is a fabulous way to embellish your garden. The right side of Figure 1-7 shows some lovely garden markers made with vintage silverware. The names of the herbs have been hand stamped onto each one. They're positively delightful!

FIGURE 1-7: Captivating TV terrarium by Heather Jeffery of Re4m (top left). Coffee bean bag plant pot covers by Helen Bradbury of Plant Apparel UK (bottom left). Silverware garden markers by Lindsay Brown of The Woodsy Way (right).

Smart storage solutions

There are scads of ways to upcycle for organization. Crates are particularly practical. You can repurpose vintage fruit or wine crates to hold shoes, toys, books, towels — you name it!

Figure 1-8 shows an example of how to stack and style crates in a foyer.

A boot bench is an inventive two-in-one idea. Made with reclaimed wood, it offers a helpful place to sit and put your boots on. It also has an open side that can house a large storage bin. Figure 1-9 shows the vibe.

Art for any space

Art and upcycling go hand in hand. Creating a gallery wall with vintage frames is a fabulous idea (see left of Figure 1-10). It's easy to find inexpensive frames from your local thrift shop, and Etsy has tons of incredible options for art prints. The right of Figure 1-10 shows the brilliant idea of framing a map.

FIGURE 1-9:
it's handy
having places
to keep large
storage bins
(left). The
perfect place
to sit and put
your boots on
(right).

FIGURE 1-10:
Gallery wall
(left) and
framed map
art by Kristine
Franklin of the
Painted Hive
(right).

Creating art with obsolete materials adds a whole new layer of intrigue to the pieces. Figure 1-11 shows some next-level art by Nick Gentry.

FIGURE 1-11:
Gorgeous upcycled art with film negatives by Nick Gentry.

Holidays decor upcycles

Upcycling is the perfect way to decorate your home for the holidays. You can find countless ways to express your creativity. The top left of Figure 1-12 shows how an old fishing minnow bucket has been transformed into a lovely seasonal display with the help of a couple great stencils.

Homemade Christmas decorations are the sweetest! The top right of Figure 1-12 shows some delightful denim trees completed to perfection with charming embroidery and cinnamon sticks.

Crafting decor is a fantastic way to upcycle fabric. The bottom left of Figure 1-12 shows a Christmas tree cushion made from a scarf, and the bottom right shows a tree-topping star made from the leftover fabric from hemmed pants.

FIGURE 1-12: Cabin Christmas bucket by Carlene Blair of Organized Clutter (top left). Denim Christmas ornaments by Vicky Myers of Vicky Myers Creations (top right). Christmas tree cushion by Colby Drover of This is Drover (bottom left). Christmas tree star by Judy Rom of Upcycle That (bottom right).

Chapter **2**
Sleuthing Out Materials

When you're ready to begin upcycling, your first step is finding materials. Luckily for you, your next great score is just around the corner. Literally. You might actually find it as you're walking down the street! The world is seemingly chock-full of items that people no longer want. This is great news for opportunistic upcyclers ready to gather the goods.

Upcycling is like a real-life treasure hunt. The objective is to scout out the finest pieces and acquire them for the best prices. Like any good adventure, there are some pitfalls to avoid. In this chapter, I explain where to consistently find the best items and how to tell if they're quality and not just, erm, actual garbage.

Go get 'em fortune seeker!

Hunting Down Materials

There are several go-to places to explore when you're looking for goodies. Here's the down-low on where to score the most prolific pieces and how to source like a professional.

A thrilling adventure: Thrift stores

There's so much opportunity to find gold at thrift stores. That said, there's a bit of an art to thrift shopping.

When you start thrift shopping it's easy to become overwhelmed or buy things you don't actually want. Here are some guidelines to make sure you can thrift shop with the best of them:

>> **Focus on finding high-quality furniture and home decor made from wood, wicker, glass, and metal.** These materials offer the best value and are the easiest to clean.

>> **Be strategic about the neighborhood that you're shopping in.** Check out the thrift stores in older neighborhoods and wealthier neighborhoods for antique and vintage finds. Over time, you'll discover which stores generally have the leading selection.

>> **Shop at the most favorable times.** To snag the choicest deals, shop when the merchandise is fresh. Mornings, Mondays, and Tuesdays are ideal because stores generally restock over the weekends.

>> **Get clear on what you're actually looking for.** Being specific about what you're after will keep you on track. Check out Chapter 19 for the top 10 things to look for at thrift stores.

>> **Shop frequently.** Committing to thrift shopping means being persistent. If you're on the hunt for something specific, devote time to visit at least weekly, and be prepared to leave empty-handed if you don't find what you're looking for.

>> **Check out lesser-known thrift stores to scoop some goodies.** The bigger chains like Salvation Army and Goodwill are often priced higher and are more picked over.

>> **Find out when the sales are.** Thrift stores offer discount days.

>> **If you see something you truly love, buy it.** The nature of thrift stores is that inventory often flips. If a unique piece catches your heart, snag it. You never know when or if you'll see it again.

TIP Frequent shoppers come out on top. If there's a thrift store by your work or home, lunch break is a great time to pop in regularly.

TIP Thrift shopping while on road trips is a perfect time to find treasures. Smaller towns and rural places often have unique items and good deals.

Figure 2-1 shows a couple of gems waiting to be discovered at a thrift shop.

FIGURE 2-1:
Here are two
thrift store
beauties
waiting to be
found.

A 24/7 opportunity: Online marketplaces

Online marketplaces like Facebook Marketplace, Craigslist, and eBay are great for when you're looking for a specific item. Another upside: they're always open. Tailor your searches by using keywords like "mid-century modern" or "farmhouse," and check frequently for the first-rate pieces. Items on here are constantly being added.

Items that are popular to buy and sell on online marketplaces include

>> **Large furniture:** This category includes couches, tables, dressers, hutches, dining room sets, and outdoor furniture.

>> **Small furniture:** Think chairs, end tables, stools, and shelves.

DESIGN STYLES

When you're reading online descriptions of marketplace items, you may see the following terms, which identify the item's design style:

- **Mid-century modern:** Simple and beautiful wooden furniture from the 1950s and '60s with a focus on clean lines and curved designs. Teak, walnut, mahogany, and rosewood were predominantly used.

- **Farmhouse:** Farmhouse style is rooted in the rustic and comfortable farmhouses of the 18th century. These items feature elements made of reclaimed wood that have been weathered or white washed.

>> **Lamps and light fixtures**: Pendant lights and chandeliers may be things you want to watch for.

>> **Seasonal decor:** Check early in the season for unique holiday decor.

>> **Rugs:** This is a reliable place to find secondhand and vintage rugs in great condition.

TIP

Buying on Facebook Marketplace is safer than buying on other online marketplaces because you can see the profile of the seller. Meet in a public place or do a "porch pickup," which means meeting in the lobby or outside the residence. If you can't do that, bring a friend with you.

TIP

Act fast if you see an item that you like. Good deals are often scooped up within the hour. Also, use the bookmark icon (see Figure 2-2) to save items that you like on Facebook Marketplace so that the service's algorithm learns your taste and can recommend relevant items.

When it comes to searching online marketplaces, the words you use matter. The descriptors and keywords you search greatly affect what you find.

Here are some keywords to search that will often deliver the literal goods:

>> **Old:** This is a good search word that often triggers undervalued vintage or antique items.

>> **Must go:** This is a surefire way to nab a great deal. Don't hesitate to negotiate here.

FIGURE 2-2:
Click the
bookmark
icon to save
an item.

>> **Grandma's/grandma/grandmother:** This frequently indicates items in pristine condition.

>> **Heavy or solid:** This is the perfect way to reference real wood furniture.

>> **Funky:** This is a great descriptor for finding unique pieces.

TIP

If you're looking for specific items, try searching using a few different terms. For instance, a couch could also be called a sofa, loveseat, daybed, or sectional. Also, when it comes to keywords, the more specific you can be the better. Try searching by decade, material, style, color, and pattern.

TIP

If you want a lower price, negotiate *before* you agree to buy the item. It always pays to be respectful when negotiating. A good tactic is to ask if the seller has any wiggle room on price. However, be mindful to avoid haggling when items are marked as "price firm."

Facebook Marketplace, Craigslist, and eBay may be the most well-known online outlets, but they're certainly not the only ones. Try checking out these other options: Kijiji, OfferUp, Nextdoor, Freecycle, and Facebook buy/sell and buy nothing groups.

The weekend mission: Garage sales

Garage sales are super fun to shop because the prices are generally low, and you truly never know what you're going to find. That being said, they can sometimes be hit-or-miss. Here's how to optimize your shopping experience.

Timing is everything

Garage sale season generally kicks off with spring cleaning and goes into the early fall. This is a weekend affair, with Saturdays from 9 a.m. to 4 p.m. being the most popular times.

When it comes to the best time of day to shop garage sales, keep these factors in mind:

>> **The early bird gets the worm.** Go at the beginning of the day to score the best pieces, especially for larger items like furniture.

>> **Midday is a good time to shop if it's super hot or rainy.** Vendors will be motivated to get out of the elements.

>> **Don't disregard the afternoon, though.** The end of the day (around 2 p.m.) is prime for scoring crazy deals because sellers are willing to slash and burn prices to get rid of things.

Planning your attack

When it comes to shopping garage sales, you can do it either organically or by researching in advance.

To find the best sales spontaneously, take the scenic route by driving through suburban neighborhoods as opposed to traveling the highways.

Shop strategically. Websites like Garage Sale Tracker and Yard Sale Search enable you to see all the advertised sales in your area. Apps like Yard Sale Treasure Map pull in listings from Craigslist. There are also a lot of local garage sale groups on Facebook. Posting in these groups regularly show images of items for sale, potentially with the option to pre-buy. Older folks (with vintage items) often advertise their garage sales in newspaper classifieds. With these tools, you can plan a route and hit multiple sales in a day.

If you don't look, you won't know

It's hard to know what's available without checking. If you drive past a garage sale, and you have time, it's worth taking a look to see what's there. You might even hit the jackpot and run into a moving sale.

When you arrive on the scene, do a loop to see what's available. Large, well-made furniture will be snatched up first.

Buying only what you truly want or love

Just because something is cheap doesn't mean it's a good deal. If you're not going to use an item or flip it, it's a waste of money.

TIP

Make a list of items you're looking for and keep it on your phone. That way you're less likely to get swept up buying things you don't need.

Scoring the lowest prices

Most of the time, garage sale prices are negotiable. Here's how to get the best deals:

>> **Bundle items:** Start a collection and offer a price for all of it or ask for a bundled discount. Sellers are motivated to sell as much as possible, so you can often get a deal on multiple items.

>> **Form a connection:** Ask about the history of the pieces and share your plans for them. People like to see their items go to a good home.

>> **Haggle within reason:** Lowballing can be seen as disrespectful. Offer a decent price (never less than 50 percent), and be prepared to negotiate up.

>> **Cash is (still) king:** Bring lots of small bills. Offering a price with cash in hand is a strong purchasing strategy.

The treasure trove: Estate sales

Estate sales or *tag sales* happen in the home of someone who has passed away or is downsizing. Everything is tagged with a price, and a third-party company or a family member generally manages the items. These sales are an incredible opportunity to find high-quality vintage and antique pieces.

Use the following steps to maximize your chance for a successful outcome when shopping an estate sale:

1. Check out www.estatesales.net to find out about upcoming sales and see preview photos of the items for sale.

2. Wait in line at the door or grab a number if an estate sale uses a number system.

3. Do a walkthrough of each room to see what's available to purchase.

4. If you find a piece you like, hold onto it and take it to the checkout. If it's a larger piece, snag the pricing ticket and take it to the host.

TIP

If you find a good estate sale, ask the hosts to put you on their email list for their upcoming sales. Also inquire whether they host estate auctions. For estate sales, photos or a preview time are often available to peruse the wares in advance. There are also online auctions on Everything But The House and eBay.

TIP

Estate sales run for 1 to 3 days, and while most items aren't up for negotiation on the first day, by the last day items are often discounted by 40 to 50 percent.

The casual score: Friends and family

When it comes to prices, you can't beat free. A great way to get free furniture is to let your family and friends know that you're looking. Make your wishes widely known by creating a post on social media. You'll be amazed at how many people have items that they'd like to rehome. It's a total win-win.

TIP

Keep an ear out for people who are moving, getting married, or have relatives who are downsizing. These are particularly opportune moments for getting free furniture.

TIP

Make it convenient for the people gifting. Offer up a few times that you're available to collect and ask them to tell you when works.

The inspirational scout: Reuse stores

Most cities have reuse stores like the ReStore that Habitat for Humanity runs. These stores receive donations of household items and building materials. The items are saved from the landfill, and the public have access to them at a reduced price. What makes these stores extra special is that the sales support housing projects around the world. It's a triple win!

The items waiting to be discovered at these stores are numerous but can include the following:

>> **Tools:** Hand tools, power tools, yard tools, shop vacs

>> **Paint:** Paint and paint supplies, including brushes

>> **New building materials:** Lumber, drywall, plywood, baseboards, bags of concrete, shelving

>> **Garden:** Landscaping brick and blocks

>> **Home exterior:** New shingles, insulation, and gutters

>> **Flooring:** New carpet, vinyl, rugs, tiles

>> **New electrical:** Light switches, wires, outlets

>> **Bathroom and plumbing supplies:** Sinks, vanities, new tubs, and medicine cabinets

>> **Hardware:** Doorknobs, hinges, pulls, fasteners

>> **Architectural items:** Mantels, stained glass, railings, spindles, columns

>> **Furniture:** Couches, chairs, hutches, bookshelves, tables and side tables, dressers, beds, office furniture, kitchen cabinets

>> **Lighting:** Table and floor lamps, sconces, chandeliers, pendants, and new bulbs and ceiling fans

>> **Home goods:** Art, mirrors, home decor

>> **Windows and doors:** Windows, shutters, and interior, exterior, and patio doors

TIP

Reuse stores are a great place to source lots of the same material, because items are often donated in bulk.

Figure 2-3 shows a great idea for building a greenhouse with lots of windows that were acquired from reuse stores.

The fortuitous find: On the street

In big cities like New York, people put out their furniture on the stoop for other people to collect. This cultural phenomenon is called *stooping*.

While the free price tag is certainly appealing, it's important to determine whether these items are roadside cash or trash. It's also imperative to search for bed bugs before picking up a piece. Be sure to reference the "Examining secondhand furniture — what to avoid" section later in this chapter for specific details.

Following are the types of pieces that you may discover during a stooping excursion:

>> Functional pieces like dressers, desks, side tables, and bookshelves

>> Items with good bones that are ripe for upcycling, like chairs you can paint and armchairs you can reupholster

TIP

Good bones refers to the overall structure and shape of the piece. You can swap out the colors and fabric of a piece, so when you're examining a potential find, focus on the structural details rather than the surface appearance.

FIGURE 2-3:
An impressive
illustration of
what can be
done with lots
of windows.

>> Shockingly beautiful pieces like glass coffee tables, velvet chairs, and claw-
foot tubs

>> Unique and unexpected fun items like movie props and chalkboards

TIP

The end of the spring semester is a great time to scoop some goodies outside col-
lege student dormitories. Dumpsters by storage facilities are another place to score
riches. People discard items here that they don't want to pay to store anymore.

TIP

If you're in New York City, follow the Instagram account @stoopingnyc for hot
tips on quality pieces.

Figure 2-4 shows some of the incredible roadside treasures that have been posted
on @stoopingnyc.

FIGURE 2-4:
An assortment
of finds posted
on the
Instagram
account
@stoopingnyc.

Knowing What to Look For (and What to Avoid!) When Sourcing

Most of the time secondhand furniture is sold as-is and isn't returnable. Because of this, properly inspecting items prior to purchasing is the single most important thing you can do.

WARNING

Also, as a good rule of thumb, avoid buying the following items secondhand:

>> Mattresses and pillows

>> Baby items like cribs and bassinets

>> Toys that can't be disinfected

>> Rugs that can't be professionally cleaned — especially if you have allergies

Examining secondhand furniture — what to look for

Here's what you're looking for when checking out furniture:

>> **Solid build:** Sturdy furniture made from solid wood with dovetailed joints demonstrates quality workmanship. Figure 2-5 shows a dovetail joint. This joinery technique doesn't require mechanical fasteners like screws.

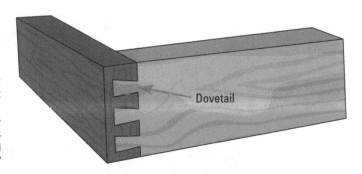

FIGURE 2-5:
A dovetail joint
is a strong join
ery technique
that interlocks
"pins" and
"tails."

Dovetail

TIP

>> **Valuable vintage:** Labels or maker's markings that can identify a piece as being vintage or antique make it more valuable. Look for the markings in or underneath drawers or at the back and lower edges of furniture.

If you locate a maker's mark, do a Google search to find out more about the brand and its possible value.

>> **Tush cush:** If it's a piece with foam, give it a squeeze. Quality foam is firm, but not too hard, and definitely not crumbly. Ideally you want to be able to work with the existing foam and not have to replace it.

>> **The allure of the quick flip:** Items that only require minimal fixes are great for quick flippers. Less time spent equals a higher profit.

>> **Unexpected treasure:** When you're shopping secondhand, you never know exactly what you'll find. Keep an open mind, especially for items that can be repurposed for something entirely new.

HOW OLD IS OLD?

Older items are classified as antique, vintage, or retro based on their age:

• **Antique**: Antique comes from the ancient French word for *old*. Items need to be at least 100 years old to be a true antique.

• **Vintage**: Vintage means "of age," and it is often used to describe the age of a wine. True vintage is thought to be 50+ years old. For furniture and home decor, vintage generally refers to items from the 1930s through the 1970s.

• **Retro**: Retro comes from the French word *retro*, to move backward (think *retrograde*). Retro items are 20+ years old. At the time I wrote this book, items from the 1980s through the early 2000s are retro.

Here are a few items that are great to buy secondhand:

>> **Solid wood, metal, glass, or wicker furniture** like dressers, desks, and headboards, especially if an item is vintage

>> **Upholstered furniture that you can have professionally cleaned** or will be reupholstered

>> **High-quality antique or vintage rugs** that you can professionally clean

Examining secondhand furniture — what to avoid

When it comes to choosing secondhand furniture, it's important to scrutinize it for damage as well as for potential hazards like bugs, mold, and toxic lead paint.

Inspecting for damage

Look out for these important factors while checking out an item for damage:

>> **Structural damage:** Give your prospect the wiggle test and look out for wobbly or broken legs and creaks. These repairs are often expensive to fix.

>> **Water damage:** You can easily sand out surface-level water damage like water rings. However, major water damage (warped panels, stuck drawers) can hint at greater problems like structural damage, wood rot, termites, and mold.

>> **Foul odors:** Steer clear of furniture that smells like body odor, urine, smoke, pets, and so on. This is particularly important for upholstered pieces, because odors are off-putting for resale buyers.

>> **Missing pieces:** Depending on the item, a missing piece may or may not be a deal breaker. Hardware is ripe for replacement, but it's important to take note of what may or may not be there (hello, all the drawers?) before committing.

>> **Condition and functionality:** Is the piece in a good, usable condition? If an item is fabric, does it have tears or stains? Inspect everything. Open and close all the drawers or sit on it if it's that kind of furniture. Bounce around on the piece as if you're using it for seating. It's important to find out if it's comfortable.

Examining for bugs

Let's not mince words here. Bed bugs are real, and they're terrifying. They're tiny, blood-sucking monsters that will keep you up all night. They're also *incredibly hard* to get rid of once you have them. *This is not a drill!* And bed bugs don't just live in the bedroom; they may be lurking on a wooden or upholstered item.

Make sure to thoroughly inspect every potential wood, fabric, or even paper item *before* bringing it anywhere near your car or home.

Bed bugs look like flat red/brownish lentils. They're great at hiding, so also look for their casings (shed skin), fecal matter, blood stains, and small holes. *If you find a bug or any evidence of them, definitely leave the item.* It's simply not worth it.

Carefully inspect the following areas:

>> Cracks and crevices of wooden furniture

>> Screw holes

>> The seams, creases, and linings of upholstered pieces

>> The drawers — remove them and look inside and underneath them

>> The bottom — flip the item over for proper inspection

Checking for mold

You don't want to bring home a piece infected with mold. Mold spores can live on wood, fabric, and upholstery and can lead to severe respiratory ailments. Watch out for that trademark musty odor, as well as any powdery patches of white, green, or black discolorations.

Looking out for lead paint

Another factor to watch out for is lead-based paint. The U.S. government banned lead paint in 1978, but prior to that year it was used extensively. Lead paint likes to peel and flake. It's dangerous to inhale or ingest lead paint chips or dust.

TIP

Identify possible lead paint by looking for wrinkled and chippy paint that resembles alligator skin. Confirm it with a DIY lead test kit that you can purchase for around $20. Keep this in your *thrift kit*. (Read about building a thrift kit in the "Building a thrift kit" section later in this chapter.

Preparing to Scour Thrift Stores

In order to score big on your thrift excursions, it's important to plan for success. Before you get going, build a thrift kit, familiarize yourself with your dimensions, and have a clear idea of what you're looking for.

Building a thrift kit

While you're thrifting, the following items are useful to have on hand. Keep these in your vehicle so they're always handy:

» Flashlight

» Magnifying glass

» Measuring tape

» Blanket/padding to cover and protect your car's upholstery when loading and unloading

» Rope and bungee cords

» Hand vacuum

» Baby wipes

» Work gloves and disposable gloves

» Screwdriver set

» Lead test kit

Knowing your space

Having the measurements of your rooms, doorways, and vehicle (trunk and inner) available while you're on the hunt is just plain practical. You never know when you'll find a great piece, and awareness of what will fit inside your space (and vehicle) is paramount.

TIP

Keep these length, width, and height dimensions on a note on your phone so they're always with you. That way, if you find a piece that's too big for your car, you'll know right away to book an UberXL!

Knowing yourself

There's a fine line between upcycling and hoarding. Potential is one thing, but knowing which projects you'll actually finish — or have the skills/budget to do — is another. Successful upcyclers consider which projects to take on and which to avoid. Have a plan of what you're looking for, and stick to a budget.

TIP

Don't get swept up just because something is cheap. A good rule of thumb is to only take items that you absolutely love. Unsure? Imagine how you would feel if someone else walked away with that piece. If you're devastated by the thought, then you know that you love the item. If you're feeling kind of ambivalent or meh, leave it for someone else.

Chapter **3**
Tapping Into Your Creativity

nspiration hits like a breath of fresh air that feeds your inner fire. In fact, the word comes from the Latin *inspirare*, which means "to breathe upon." The breath of inspiration fuels the creative passion that lights you up!

But what happens when you're not feeling inspired? What do you do when the guiding gale force isn't blowing? Well, as it turns out, you *can* coax it along. There are lots of ways to find vision and get your artistic juices flowing.

In this chapter, I suggest ways to spark your powerful, imaginative energy. You'll gain an understanding of where to look for inspiration and how to capture it. This includes cataloging ideas on your phone, searching Pinterest and Instagram, and making digital or physical mood boards. Finally, you'll experience the fun of selecting color schemes and gain the benefit of sketching out your vision *before* painting it.

Getting Inspired

You might not realize it just yet, but inspiration is everywhere! From the bold color combination of an outfit to a breathtaking sunset, if it catches your eye, there's something to it.

Once you see something that speaks to you, the trick is to seize the moment in a way that you can revisit. Read on for how.

Discovering inspiration in the world

While going about your day, always be on the lookout for things that turn your head and awaken your spirit.

TIP

The camera on your phone is great for capturing spontaneous moments. Keep a folder in your phone's gallery for photos that ignite you. That way it's easy to find and flip through them whenever you want a hit of inspiration.

Browsing Pinterest

Pinterest is an excellent resource for finding inspiration online. The content that you save (like photos, projects, products, videos, and guides) are called *pins*. Your home feed shows you pins from accounts that you follow, as well as suggested content that it thinks you'll like.

You can also find goodies through the Pinterest search bar. Try typing "upcycled furniture ideas" or "repurposed furniture" to see what pops up.

Figure 3-1 shows an example of a board created from photos found on Pinterest. It's like a digital mood board for cataloging inspiration that you see. It's a great way to figure out what design aesthetic or "vibe" you like. Think of it as a creative launch pad. You can create boards with whatever theme you want and return to them in the future.

TIP

Try making boards for desirable color combos or for inspiring upcycling projects. You can upload pins to your boards via the Pinterest app or website on your phone or computer.

If you want to save photos directly from the webpage that you find the inspiration on, first enable the Pinterest browser button. Go to your browser's store (for example, the Chrome Web Store) to find and download it. This button is a savvy tool for saving ideas because when you pin this way, the photos you save on Pinterest link back to the original website. Figure 3-2 shows how easy it is to click to save a pin once you've enabled this feature.

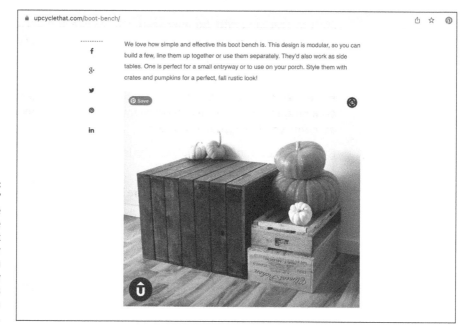

Browsing Instagram

Instagram is another helpful resource for finding inspiration. Seeing what other upcyclers and makers are creating can motivate you and give you lots of ideas. Types of accounts that I recommend following include:

- **Upcyclers** like my own account, @upcyclethat who post inspiring photos and projects

- **Industry leaders** who share upcycle trends and tutorials

- **Photographers** who post unique and interesting pictures of nature, travel, and fashion that can inspire color combos for upcycling

- **Businesses** like paint companies that offer similar or complementary products

TIP

Check out the Instagram Search & Explore page to see suggested posts based on the accounts you follow and images you've liked.

Using the search bar

You can discover worthy accounts on Instagram by searching for topics and hashtags. Here's how:

1. **Tap the magnifying glass to get to the search bar.**

2. **Start by searching with broader search terms like #upcycling and then narrow the search to niche areas that interest you specifically, like #upcyclingfurniture, #upcycledfurnitureforsale, and #upcycledhomedecor.**

3. **In the feed of pictures tagged with that hashtag that pops up, you can click on specific images to enlarge them and choose to follow the accounts you find visually appealing.**

   Figure 3-3 shows an example of how the feed might look for #upcycledfurniture.

4. **Check out the related hashtags (on the right of Figure 3-3) that pop up in the search results to get more ideas.**

Saving posts on Instagram

You can save chosen Instagram posts to collections so you can keep track of inspiring photos and videos. It's also a brilliant way to start noticing patterns about the type of visual trends you find appealing. Then you can incorporate these styles into your own work.

TIP

Making digital mood boards is simple and free on Canva.com (`https://canva.com`). Type **mood board** into the search bar and use one of their templates. Figure 3-5 shows an example of a farmhouse-style mood board made on Canva.

FIGURE 3-5:
A mood board made on Canva with images discovered through Pinterest.

Here's one method for making your own mood board:

1. **Brainstorm the keywords that describe the vibe/aesthetic of your project.**

2. **Decide if you want to make a physical or a digital mood board.**

3. **For a physical mood board, locate magazine photos and fabric scraps that evoke your desired feeling and glue them on a big piece of paper in an appealing way.**

4. **For a digital mood board, take images that you've saved on your phone or Pinterest and arrange them in a lovely composition on Canva.**

Working with Color Schemes

Ideally you want to have a sense of what colors you're going to use before you start painting your furniture.

TIP

The classic way to experiment with color combinations is with a color wheel. Figure 3-6 shows examples of the following color schemes:

» **Monochromatic:** Using only one hue, such as blue, and adding tints (with white paint) and shades (with black paint).

» **Analogous:** Picking a dominant color and then using its adjacent colors as accents, similar to a sunset or a rainbow.

» **Triad:** Picking your dominant color and then accenting it with two other colors that are evenly distanced on the color wheel.

» **Complementary:** Selecting the color directly on the other side of the color wheel.

» **Split-complementary:** Choosing two shades equally spaced away. This is a softer look than complementary.

» **Tetradic or double-complementary:** Including two sets of complementary colors. A daring choice.

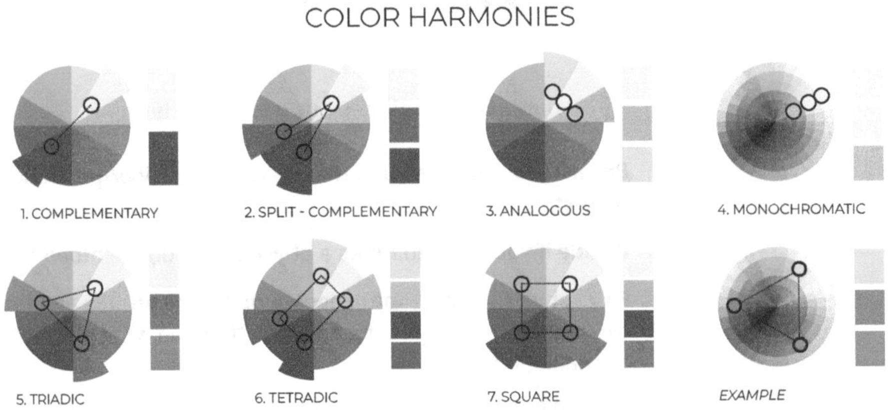

COLOR HARMONIES

1. COMPLEMENTARY 2. SPLIT - COMPLEMENTARY 3. ANALOGOUS 4. MONOCHROMATIC

FIGURE 3-6:
Some color schemes from the color wheel you might like to use.

5. TRIADIC 6. TETRADIC 7. SQUARE *EXAMPLE*

Other than using a color wheel, you can play with color combinations using paint swatches from the hardware store or a free, online palette creator. I recommend using Coolors (`https://coolors.co`). Figure 3-7 shows a palette made on Coolors. You can find this tool at Tools ⇨ Palette Generator on the Coolors site.

The Image Converter tool, available on the Tools menu on Coolors, is ideal for picking up colors from within an image you upload, like an eyedropper. It's a useful tool for experimenting with how colors work together.

FIGURE 3-7: A palette made using the Image Converter on Coolors with an image of Moroccan plates from Raúl Cacho Osús found on Unsplash.com.

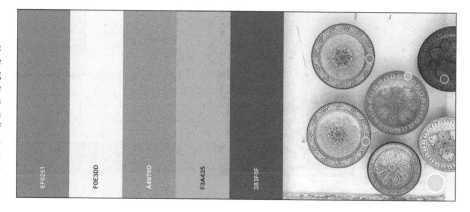

Unsplash.com is a good place to search and find beautiful images. This is a good option if you're looking for more places to find visual inspiration.

Sketching Your Vision

Once you have an idea of the colors you want to use, you can do a rough sketch of your furniture piece and try painting colors on it to see how they'll look once they're applied. Figure 3-8 shows an example.

Draw a rough sketch of your piece and photocopy it so you can try painting multiple variations onto your sketches. Use your favorite elements from these sketches to create your upcycled piece.

If you prefer to experiment digitally, you can use the free Benjamin Moore Color Viewer tool (`https://benjaminmoore.com/en-us/color-overview/personal-color-viewer`) to experiment with "painting" colors on an image of your piece, as I've done on the chest of drawers in Figure 3-9.

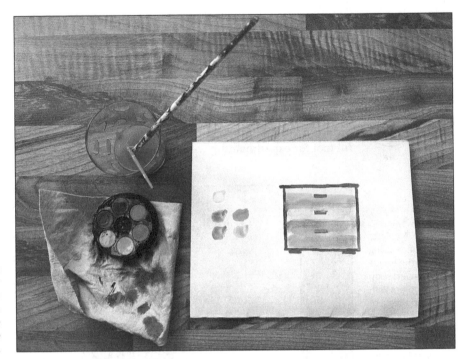

FIGURE 3-8: Painting over sketches is a great way to visualize how the piece will look.

FIGURE 3-9: Digital color sketching on the Benjamin Moore Color Viewer tool, using an image by Rumman Amin from Unsplash.com.

2

The Big Upcycle: Preparing and Painting Your Piece

Get skilled in how to properly prepare your piece by cleaning, sanding, and priming it before painting.

Gather the right kinds of brushes and paint and figure out how to use them.

Explore different techniques for adding rustic charm and aging effects without having to wait for decades.

Elevate your upcycle with fun and functional hardware.

Master the art of restoring and refinishing furniture to its full glory.

Chapter 4

Preparing Your Piece for Transformation

Y ou've just scored an incredible wooden furniture piece, and you're jazzed to repaint it. Awesome! Painting wood furniture is an effective way to transform it. However, before you break out the brush, you need to take care of a few things first.

If you're wondering what sets a good upcycle apart from a great one, the answer is preparation. Prepping your piece gives it the professional finish that stands the test of time. Don't skip this step! If you cut corners here, you'll end up with a chippy and paint peeling *disaster.* And then you'll have to strip it all off and start over again. You don't want that. Cleaning, sanding, and priming definitely take some time, but they set the foundation for a high-quality finish. This is what pays off in the end — especially if you can flip and resell your upcycle for double or triple what you paid.

In this chapter, I suggest what tools and materials to use for cleaning, sanding, and priming. I explain how to do these steps so that your project is properly prepped for painting. This chapter helps you avoid common mistakes and ensures that you're set up for success. By following these steps, you'll end up with a gorgeous piece that'll look stunning for years to come.

Gathering Your Tools and Materials

Before beginning, make sure you have the equipment that you need. You don't want to have to stop in the middle of a project to run out to the store.

Cleaning

You'll likely already have most of the things that you need for cleaning. A mixture of warm water with a squirt or two of dish soap and a sponge or rag is effective for most pieces, or you can buy a grease remover if there is a heavily shellacked finish that requires stripping. An old toothbrush is perfect for tidying up little nooks and crannies.

Have these cleaning supplies at the ready:

>> Dish soap

>> Sponge/cleaning cloth/rag/scouring pad

>> Old toothbrush

>> Bucket with clean, warm water

>> Natural cleaning solution such as one part vinegar to three parts water in a spray bottle for chemical-free cleaning

>> Grease remover like mineral spirits, denatured alcohol, liquid TSP, or Krud Kutter (optional)

>> Gloves (especially important if you're using a chemical cleaning solvent)

>> Shop vac or vacuum for vacuuming out drawers

Sanding

You can sand a piece in a low-fi way with sandpaper and a sanding block, or you can upgrade to an electrical sander. Electrical sanders offer excellent bang for your buck. They're reasonably priced (around $100) and will save you so much time and effort.

Sanding creates a lot of dust, so some materials I've listed are for safety reasons as well as for cleaning up:

>> A variety of sandpaper grits (see the sandpaper grit guide in Table 4-1)

>> Sanding block/sponge

- » Electrical sander

- » Mask

- » Safety glasses

- » Shop vac

- » Putty knife

- » Wood filler

- » Tack cloth

Sandpaper comes in different grits that are designated by a number. The higher the number, the finer the grit. And the finer the grit you use when sanding, the smoother the sanded surface will be. Table 4-1 gives you a rundown of grits and when to use each one.

TABLE 4-1   **Sandpaper Grit Guide**

Sandpaper Grit	Grit Range	Ideal Use
Coarse	60–80 grit	Shaping wood, such as rounding corners; heavy stripping when there's chipping paint or a textured finish
Medium	100–150 grit	Removing old paint and surface levelling
Fine	180–240 grit	Smoothing out a finish, prepping for chalk paint
Extra Fine	320–400 grit	In between coats of paint and final finish

Priming

With the exception of chalk paint, which doesn't require it, *primer* is a base coat that you apply before painting your furniture piece. It's a special kind of paint that prepares your furniture to receive the paint. The primer improves the paint's durability and adhesion and stops the paint from peeling. It also stops the wood grain from "bleeding through" or appearing from beneath your paint like the ghost of Christmas past.

The following are the supplies you need for priming:

- » Painter's tape

- » Primer

>> Mini-foam roller

>> Angled sash brush

>> Rubber gloves

>> Mask

TIP

Wearing a mask while priming and painting reduces your exposure to the chemicals contained within these products.

Cleaning 101

Every good upcycle needs to start with a solid cleaning. Furniture tends to be dirty, especially when you find an item curbside. Even if a piece just came from a friend's home, you probably still need to clean it. Furniture collects dirt, dust, oils, spills, and grease. This grime makes it hard for paint to adhere, so it's imperative to remove it.

TIP

Here's how to clean wood furniture:

1. **Remove the hardware (handles and hinges), drawers, knobs, cushions, and mirrors.**

   Vacuum the inside of the drawers (if applicable).

2. **Wipe down the piece with a sponge and the cleaner of your choice.**

3. **Wipe it again with a clean sponge and water.**

4. **Allow time to air dry completely.**

   Let the furniture dry thoroughly before you start sanding. This is essential to ensure a good finish on your paint job.

TIP

If you're reusing the hardware, clean it while you're waiting for the furniture to dry. Soak it in a hot, soapy bucket, and then rinse and dry it.

REMEMBER

It's important to clean *before* sanding to avoid grinding built-up grime into the grain of the wood.

Sanding 101

"Oh, I can't wait to sand!" said no one ever. Look, it's true that sanding is a bit of a mission, and it's messy. You're probably tempted to skip this step, but the truth is that 9 times out of 10, it's necessary. Even if you're using chalk paint, still scuff up the surface to ensure proper paint adhesion.

Sanding doesn't have to be a big deal. This section explains why sanding is important, tells how best to do it, and offers some examples of when you actually don't need to sand.

Recognizing why sanding is your friend

In a nutshell, sanding allows for your paint to adhere to the wood. It takes the glossy finish off the wood so that your paint has something to grab onto. If you skip this step, you risk your paint peeling and chipping off. Then you'll have to strip it and start all over again, which ends up being a lot more work. Sanding facilitates a smooth paint finish, and it allows you to take care of any dimples or imperfections in your wood.

TIP

This is a good time to see if your furniture needs any repairs. Are there any dings, holes, or cracks in the wood? If so, use your putty brush to apply wood filler, allow time to dry, and then sand it smooth. Pro tip: Use these same steps for filling in old hardware holes.

Smoothing your way to master sander status

Sanding doesn't have to be overwhelming. You're not looking to strip the whole surface down to bare wood. You mainly want to rough it up a bit to dull the previous paint's gloss. This gives your fresh paint something to sink its teeth into.

Medium-grit sandpaper, like 150 grit, is perfect for this. (Refer to Table 4-1 earlier in this chapter for more information on grit.) A sandpaper block works in a pinch, but an orbital sander is even better. Orbital sanders are handheld, electric sanders that have a circular, oscillating pad that sandpaper mounts onto. They're inexpensive and easy to use and will cut your sanding time down substantially. Orbital sanders are versatile for many upcycle jobs and are definitely worth buying. A corner cat sander is also a great, complementary purchase. It has a wedge shape (like an iron) that's perfect for those tight corners that an orbital sander can't get into. Figure 4-1 shows these two electric sanders.

When sanding, be sure to swap out your sanding paper if it wears smooth or gets clogged up with dust. Practice patience while sanding and remember not to press too hard, or you'll risk gouging the wood. The best technique is to keep the sander flat, go in the direction of the grain, and let the sander glide along without forcing it.

FIGURE 4-1:
Different sanding tools: a corner cat sander (left) and an orbital sander (right).

A sanding block is better than loose sandpaper because it allows you to exert pressure. A sanding sponge is ideal for use on curved surfaces. A cut pool noodle with sandpaper wrapped around it makes a great sanding pad for rounded surfaces.

Going against the grain can leave ghastly scratches. Always sand with the grain, using long and even strokes.

Cleaning up the dust storm

Sanding creates a *lot* of dust, and the dust goes *everywhere*. This is a big reason people hate to sand. But when you know how to handle the mess, sanding becomes just another step in the process of upcycling.

Wear a mask and goggles when you sand to protect your eyes and nose, mouth, and lungs. Sanding outside (if possible) or in a workshop is great because you have less mess to clean up. If you're inside, use a shop vac to vacuum up the sanding dust on and around your piece. Then finish it off by using a tack cloth to remove the sanding residue. A tack cloth has a sticky finish that's like a magnet for dust. Don't skip this step. It saves you from having the paint equivalent of ingrown hairs.

If you're in a pinch and don't have tack cloth, you can use a damp cloth, followed by a dry one to remove dust residue. However, a tack cloth really is best.

Knowing when you can skip sanding

Although sanding is generally the key to ensuring a professional paint finish, there are times when you're able to skip it — like when using chalk, mineral, or milk paint. Chalk paint offers a lovely matte finish and is a great option to paint just about anything without sanding first. As a fun bonus, it also turns your furniture into a chalkboard! Learn more about different paint options in Chapter 5.

There are also scenarios in which your item might have detailed carving too intricate to sand. In that case, you have other options to dull the paint's surface. For your paint to stick, you can use a liquid sander or deglosser. You apply a deglosser with rubber gloves and a rag, and it does exactly what it sounds like: It removes the paint's shiny surface.

A deglosser is a chemical solution, so wear protective gloves and goggles and ideally work outside. Be sure to read the instructions on your brand's deglosser in terms of how long to leave it on, and then wipe it up with a clean, wet rag.

If you're going to go the no-sand route, it's worth doing a test: Paint a small patch, let it dry, and then make a small scratch to see if it peels off.

Priming 101

When your project is dry and dust-free, it's prime time! *Primer* is a special kind of paint that acts as a base coat. It helps your paint hold fast, and it lends itself to better coverage and durability. This is especially helpful if you're painting lighter colors over dark. Figure 4-2 shows some good all-purpose primers.

If you don't prime, knots in the wood can show through as dark spots. This is called *bleeding through*, and it's about as fun as it sounds.

FIGURE 4-2:
These primers
work well for
paint adhesion.

TIP

Here's how to prime:

1. **Apply painter's tape to protect areas that you don't want to paint, such as drawer edges.**

2. **Apply a thin coat of primer in the direction of the grain with a mini-foam roller.**

   An angled, a long-handled brush with angled bristles, is great for getting into corners.

3. **Allow the coat of primer to dry.**

4. **Lightly sand with 220-grit sandpaper.**

   Sanding between coats of primer helps ensure that you have an even finish with your end result.

5. **Apply a second coat.**

6. **Allow it to fully dry.**

7. **Lightly sand with 220-grit sandpaper, making sure to sand away any drips.**

8. **Remove the dust with a tack cloth.**

   You're now ready for painting!

Chapter **5**

Sprucing Up Your Furniture Piece

E veryone loves a good transformation. When it comes to furniture flipping, painting is the ultimate metamorphosis. Nothing revitalizes furniture quite like a fresh coat of paint!

When done right, painting furniture offers major potential upsides and soaring levels of personal satisfaction. However, without proper guidance, it can be tedious, frustrating, and downright messy.

In this chapter, I share the secret sauce of painting furniture — what order to paint in, which tools and materials are best, and the exact techniques to use. Get ready for the glow up!

Painting in Proper Sequence

If you want to be a proficient painter, follow these steps:

1. Cleaning: It's *essential* to clean your piece before painting. Refer to Chapter 4 for the specifics.

2. Sanding: You need to rough up the surface to help the paint adhere. Sanding isn't strictly necessary for chalk paint, but a light five-minute sand is a good call. Chapter 4 goes into more detail on sanding.

3. Priming: A coat of primer helps your paint adhere long term and prevents bleed-through. Certain paints don't require priming. Chapter 4 provides clarity on when and how to use primer.

4. Painting: Select the right paintbrushes and paint for your project. The section below details how.

5. Sanding between coats: After your paint has dried, use a fine-grit sandpaper like 320 grit to lightly sand the piece. This smooths your finish and removes any visible brushstrokes and paint drips. Remove the sanding dust with a tack cloth.

6. Sealing with a topcoat: You need to seal certain paint with a topcoat to ensure long-term durability. Chapter 6 goes into the specifics of working with sealants.

Gathering Your Tools and Materials

Choosing the right tools and paint enables you to elevate your project to the next level. Here's the rundown of who's who in the hardware store.

Brushes

Brushes can make or break your project. Streaky lines? No thanks. With so many brushes to choose from, it can be tricky to know which ones to pick. Here are some factors to consider when making your selections:

TIP

>> **Your budget:** Although you get what you pay for with brushes, you don't have to start with the top of the line. Use what you can afford, and invest in quality brushes as your project frequency increases.

>> **The number of projects you plan to do:** If you're only going to do a few projects, you don't need the crème de la crème. However, if you plan to upcycle as a business, you'll want to invest in professional brushes.

Higher quality brushes last longer and provide value over multiple projects.

TIP

>> **The product that you're using:** If you're using an oil-based paint or applying stripper, it doesn't make sense to use an expensive brush that will get wrecked. For one-time uses, choose inexpensive chip brushes. Originally

designed for brushing wood chips away from machines, these inexpensive brushes are perfect for applying harsher solvents. Pick them up at any hardware store for a couple of bucks.

Because chip brushes often loose bristles, it makes sense to wash (and shed) them before using. Run cold water over the brush, getting it into the base of the bristles. Squeeze the bristles in your fist to work the water in. Then, dry the brush by spinning the handle in between your hands until it's only slightly damp.

>> **Natural versus synthetic:** Natural bristles are coarser and therefore more likely to leave brushstrokes. This is great for a textured look like farmhouse (refer to Chapter 2 for an explanation of this design style) or when you need a rigid brush, like with waxing. Synthetic brushes are softer and leave a smoother finish. They're made from polyester and nylon.

>> **The handle:** The more comfortable the handle is, the smoother the results will be. Long handles can effortlessly reach back corners. Conversely, short handles offer more maneuverability; they're best for getting into tight spots.

>> **The right size and shape for the job:** To cover larger areas, bring in a larger brush or a paint roller. For smaller spaces (or for intricate details) work with a smaller brush. Table 5-1 gives you a rundown of paintbrush size and shape and when is ideal to use each. Figure 5-1 illustrates the different brush shapes.

A larger brush is better for greater surfaces because it can cover ground in fewer strokes, saving time and reducing the possibility of visible brush marks.

It's handy to have a few different styles of brushes and rollers to use for different projects. Using a paint roller saves you a lot of time when painting large surfaces like dressers. Use a brush to get into the crevices that the roller can't reach, and then roll out the rest.

TABLE 5-1

Paintbrush Shape Guide

Shape	Size	Ideal use
Straight/flat	2" – 4"	Flat, large surface area
Angled	1" – 2"	Corners and grooves
Oval/round	1.25" – 1.75"	Decorative finishes, blending, waxing
Pointed/French tip	0.75" – 1.5"	Curved and detailed edges, like legs

FIGURE 5-1:
Different
paintbrush
shapes from
left to right:
straight,
angled, oval,
pointed.

Proper paintbrush care

Be sure to wash your brushes thoroughly after using them, and don't forget to reshape them and lay them flat to dry. This maintains their condition. A drop of dish soap and lukewarm water is effective for cleaning water-based paint from brushes. Work the suds through the bristles and rinse until the water runs clear.

For oil-based paints, you need to soak the brushes in mineral spirits for a few minutes and then brush the bristles out with a paintbrush comb. Repeat the soaking and combing as many times as necessary. Then wash the brush with soap and water as you would for cleaning up water-based paints.

TIP

Do not wash your brushes in hot water because doing so can ruin your brushes. Hot water can cause any remaining paint to clot to the bristles, and it also ruins the adhesive that holds the bristles in place.

TIP

Between coats, you can place your brushes in a plastic sealable bag so that the paint doesn't dry and clump up in the bristles. It can last a good couple of days like this if necessary.

Types of paint

It's easy to feel overwhelmed when perusing the paint aisle; there are so many different kinds of furniture paint! No need to stress, Table 5-2 breaks down the types and their important-to-know features.

TABLE 5-2   ## Furniture Paint Guide

Paint	Description	Usage Details	Good to Know
Chalk paint	Made with talc, calcium carbonate, and pigment, chalk paint is water-based with low volatile organic compounds (VOCs), which means it's not smelly.	Doesn't require sanding prior to application. Great for wood or metal furniture. Dries fast with a matte finish. Ideal for achieving a shabby chic look.	Can be used to turn any furniture piece into a chalkboard. Thicker by nature than all other paints, meaning it offers great coverage in fewer coats. Easy to seal with wax or poly. Can be used to paint upholstery.
Milk paint	This water-based paint is made with eco-friendly and natural ingredients like milk protein casein (hence the name), clay, and limestone. It has low VOCs and a thinner texture than chalk paint.	Also known as "chippy paint" because it flakes, so it's best for a distressed look on wooden furniture where you want to have a lot of patina — e.g., farmhouse style.	Comes in a powder form that you need to mix with water before use. Doesn't require sanding prior to application, although you definitely want to seal it to preserve the look. Thinner than chalk paint, so it requires more coats. Use a milk paint bonding agent (a concentrated water-based acrylic emulsion) for increased saturation on smooth surfaces. The amount of chipping is unpredictable.
Acrylic	This water-based paint is made with pigment and acrylic polymer.	This affordable paint offers a rich color and smooth finish. It is resistant to chipping when applied on top of primer and properly sealed.	Because this paint is water based, you can easily clean wet paint with soap and water. Cannot be applied over a surface that previously had oil-based paint unless you've stripped it.
Mineral	For this paint, natural minerals are mixed with a binder and a solvent.	Offers fantastic adhesion, a smooth finish, and durability without priming or sanding.	More expensive, but offers a top-notch finish and saves a lot of time and effort.

(continued)

TABLE 5-2 *(continued)*

Paint	Description	Usage Details	Good to Know
Oil-based or alkyd paint	This old-school oil-based furniture paint is the most durable of the furniture paints. It's ideal for high-traffic areas.	Can be used on most surfaces, including metal. Takes a long time to dry and needs lots of ventilation because it's high in VOCs.	Requires mineral spirits or turpentine for clean-up. Can be applied over surfaces previously painted with either oil-based or water-based paints. Doesn't necessarily need a topcoat. White oil-based paint has a tendency to yellow over time.
Latex paint	This water-based paint offers a smooth finish that you can use on a variety of surfaces.	Easy to find and comes in a variety of colors and finishes. Dries fast but cures slow and soft, which means it's easy to scratch. Needs to be used with primer and sealant to increase longevity.	Affordability is the main reason to choose latex paint. It's water-based, so you can clean it with soap and water.
Acrylic-alkyd	This type of paint is a hybrid water-based version of alkyd paint (which was traditionally oil-based).	Offers the smooth and durable finish of an oil-based paint but with a faster drying time and easier cleanup.	The best of both worlds for latex and oil-based paint. Cures faster than latex paint with much lower VOCs than oil-based paint.
Spray paint	Spray paint is easy to use and adheres to most surfaces.	Ideal for when you want a high-gloss look without brushstrokes.	Produces a lot of fumes, so you'll need to work outside and with a mask. Needs time to off-gas (release the chemicals in vapor form) before the odor goes away and the item is safe to bring inside. The cans don't hold that much paint, so buy a few spare and return any extras that you don't end up using.

Understanding the Painting Process

Follow these easy instructions to paint like a pro:

1. **Set up your workspace.**

   Make sure to work in a well-ventilated and well-lit space. Lay down drop cloths to protect your floors from paint drips.

2. **Plan for success.**

   Take a moment to consider your best plan of attack for painting in terms of which order you should paint what.

3. **Stir the paint thoroughly.**

   Ensure the consistency is right and the color is well blended by carefully stirring the paint before you start applying it.

4. **Dip your paintbrush into the paint halfway up the bristles.**

   Wipe off the excess paint so that it's not dripping off.

5. **Use long brushstrokes.**

   Paint from end to end in the direction of the wood grain to reduce visible brushstrokes.

6. **Let each coat of paint dry fully before applying additional coats.**

   Lightly sand (to remove imperfections) and clean with a tack cloth prior to adding another coat.

TIP

Less is more when it comes to using paint. Overloading your brush leads to paint drips. Plan to paint two to three thin coats for smooth, even coverage.

REMEMBER

Paint from one side of the piece to the other with long strokes and then let it dry fully before painting the area again. Avoid brushing back and forth multiple times as this leads to visible brushstrokes.

TIP

Watch out for paint drips. If you notice a drip while the paint is still wet, brush it out. If it's already starting to dry and is tacky, let it dry completely and then scrape or sand it off and repaint the area.

Becoming Familiar with Painting Techniques

Painting is where the upcycling magic happens! It's one of the most fun parts. The following sections include some of my top techniques.

Painting perfect lines

Painting crisp and clean lines is oh-so-satisfying! Use painter's tape to get perfectly straight lines. Figure 5-2 shows the kind of designs you can achieve with this technique.

FIGURE 5-2:
Precision lines
on a gorgeous
desk by Judy
Rom of Upcycle
That.

Painting perfect lines isn't difficult, but it requires some preparation and patience. Chapter 12 features a Chevron-Inspired Desk that details the steps.

Creating an ombre effect

An ombre is a gorgeous, gradient color effect where two or more colors are gradually blended into each other. The left side of Figure 5-3 shows a side table that's been painted with the ombre technique. (Read about the process from start to finish in Chapter 12.)

FIGURE 5-3:
This side table by Judy Rom looks beautiful with an ombre design (left). The two paints used (right).

TIP

The simplest ombre would be with two colors only, but you can easily include a third color by blending equal parts of the two shades of paint. It's easiest to blend colors that are similar or at least in the same color tone.

Here are the supplies you need to paint an ombre:

>> Paint roller

>> Two or more paint colors

>> Paintbrushes

>> Painter's tray or palette

TIP

You need to keep each color separate. You don't want to accidentally contaminate your entire paint pot with a blended shade.

>> Misting bottle

Here's how to create an ombre:

1. **Apply a base coat before you start blending.**

   Paint your colors in their sections. So, if you are doing two colors, divide your piece into two sections and paint the colors accordingly.

2. **Add a second layer of the base coat (if necessary).**

3. **Pour the two colors side by side into your paint tray or onto your palette.**

   Position the paints in the order they appear on your piece. The right of Figure 5-3 shows how to load the paint onto your roller for blending.

4. **Roll your paint roller into the two colors as shown.**

   Start with a light amount of paint so you don't oversaturate the roller.

5. **Roll to blend.**

   Pass the roller back and forth over the area to blend. You can move the roller up or down slightly to mingle the colors together. If the paint starts to dry, spray it lightly with your misting bottle.

6. **Smooth the roller strokes with your paintbrush (if necessary).**

TIP

Work on one section at a time. So, if you have a three-color ombre, focus on blending the bottom section before moving onto the top section.

Creating Interest with Papers and Designs

The difference between a good upcycle and a great one is in the details. When you're looking to add intrigue, consider using stencils, wallpapers, and decoupage.

Stencils

Stencils are an excellent way to add charming detail. The stunning entertainment console on the left in Figure 5-4 is elevated by its stenciled pattern. The right side of Figure 5-4 shows a lovely, cobalt blue stencil inspired by fine china.

TIP

Once you get the hang of it, stencils are really rewarding. They're also economical. With proper cleaning and storage, you can reuse them again and again.

FIGURE 5-4:
Kristine Franklin of the Painted Hive created the gorgeous piece on the left. Stephanie Jones of Me & Mrs. Jones made the stunning dresser on the right.

Here are the tools and supplies you need for stenciling:

>> **Stencil(s):** You can find so many amazing designs online or at your local craft store.

>> **Adhesive:** Hold the stencil in place with either painter's tape or spray adhesive.

>> **Stenciling brush:** A round brush with a flat head is ideal.

>> **Paint:** Thicker paints like chalk paint or chalk paste work great.

>> **Scrap paper or rag:** You offload the paint onto a piece of scrap paper or a rag.

Offloading means removing the excess paint by patting it onto a rag or onto scrap paper. The brush should be almost dry to the touch. This is the key to creating crisp stencils without bleed-through.

Use the following steps to apply the stencil:

1. **Prep the area.**

   Clean, sand, and prime (if necessary) the area so it's ready to receive the paint.

2. **Paint the base coat.**

   A base coat is optional. You may prefer to stencil directly onto the wood.

3. **Decide where you want the stencil to go.**

4. **Stabilize the stencil.**

   Spray adhesive directly onto the back of the stencil and place it, or secure it with painter's tape. Spray adhesive is ideal because it eliminates the potential for bleed-through. To use it: spray the adhesive onto the stencil and allow it a minute to get tacky before placing it where you'd like.

5. **Dip the paintbrush into paint and offload it.**

6. **Paint with a tapping motion.**

   Dab the paintbrush up and down.

7. **Let the paint dry according to its own instructed drying time, and then paint a second coat.**

   You can save yourself time by leaving the stencil in place between coats.

8. **Match up the stencil design to cover larger areas.**

   Make sure to let the first section dry before you do an overlapping section. Line up the stencil as best as you can and then secure it in place before painting.

TIP

   If you're painting around edges (think drawer edges), bend the stencil and hold it in place as you paint. If you're painting into corners, place the stencil over the top and dab right into the corner. You might have to touch up the area around it.

9. **Touch up the area with an artist's paintbrush.**

10. **Clean your stencil.**

   When you're done with your stencil, make sure to clean it thoroughly before storing it. This is important to its longevity.

11. **Seal the piece to protect your design.**

   Read about sealing in Chapter 6.

REMEMBER

The key to crisp stencils is working with an almost dry brush. Be sure to offload excess paint before you start applying it onto your surface.

Wallpapers

Upcyclers in the know recognize that wallpapers aren't just for walls. Wallpaper is a great way to add an interesting pop to drawer inlays, the sides of pieces, or drawers fronts, such as in Figure 5-5.

Wallpapering furniture is actually easier than wallpapering walls because the surface areas are much smaller. It's also way less expensive because you don't need as much wallpaper.

There are two kinds of wallpaper:

>> **Pasted wallpaper:** You mix and apply wallpaper paste to the wallpaper prior to using it.

>> **Adhesive wallpaper:** The wallpaper is self-backed, like a sticker.

To apply wallpaper, you need the following supplies:

>> Wallpaper

>> Adhesive/paste (if using pasted wallpaper)

>> Paint roller (for applying the paste)

>> Scraper

>> Hobby knife (like an X-Acto)

The techniques for applying pasted wallpaper and adhesive wallpaper are slightly different.

Applying pasted wallpaper

Use the following steps to apply pasted wallpaper to your piece:

1. **Prepare the paste according to the directions on the package.**

   Be sure to mix it thoroughly.

2. **Cut your paper and leave three extra inches at both the top and the bottom.**

   TIP

   It's helpful to label "top" and "bottom" or "left" and "right" onto the back of your wallpaper so you remember which side goes where.

3. **Roll the paste directly to the back of the paper and let it soak in for the instructed amount of time.**

   TIP

   The easiest way to apply the paste is to lay your wallpaper on a flat surface and roll the adhesive on with a foam roller.

4. **Line up the wallpaper where you want to place it.**

5. **Push air bubbles out to the side with your scraper.**

6. **Cut off the paper with the hobby knife and a straight edge.**

7. **If you're using more than one wallpaper panel, repeat steps 2–6.**

Applying adhesive wallpaper

Use the following steps to apply adhesive wallpaper to your piece:

1. **Clean the furniture.**

   Cleaning is always an important step, but it's extra essential when working with adhesive wallpaper because you want the adhesive to stick to the furniture, not grimy buildup!

2. **Trim your paper and leave wiggle room — three extra inches for the top and three extra for the bottom.**

3. **Remove a bit of the backing at a time.**

   This is a handy technique to help you line up the position of the wallpaper perfectly. Gradually remove more of the backing and smooth out the wrinkles as you go.

   If you have an air bubble that just won't quit, use your sharp knife to make a tiny hole to pop it.

4. **Line up and repeat the process for any additional panels.**

5. **Cut off the wallpaper at the edge with a sharp blade and a ruler.**

If you're wallpapering the front of a drawer, you can sand on top of the edges to remove excess wallpaper and leave a nice crisp line.

Decoupage

Decoupage is when you glue paper or fabric onto the surface of your piece. You can use wrapping paper, tissue paper, napkins, tinfoil . . . the options are endless.

Decoupage can really level up your pieces. The detail on the chest in Figure 5-6 adds extra oomph!

Gather the following supplies for your decoupage project:

>> Decoupage adhesive

>> Decoupage papers

>> Paintbrush

>> Scissors

>> Roller or squeegee

>> Furniture paint (optional)

>> Sealant

Mod Podge is a popular choice for a decoupage adhesive.

Decoupaging is a wonderful opportunity for experimenting with different materials. Be aware that different materials handle differently. For example, thinner paper tends to wrinkle more easily.

FIGURE 5-6:
The vintage floral paper used to decoupage this handmade chest gives a brand-new piece an aged look.

When you're ready to get started, follow these steps:

1. **Prepare the surface.**

   At a minimum, give the area a light sand. Consider painting a basecoat because most thin decoupage papers go somewhat translucent.

2. **Plan where you want the papers to go.**

   Hold them up to your piece to see how they'll look.

3. **Cut the items to fit.**

4. **Apply the adhesive directly to the surface.**

5. **Add your papers and smooth out any air bubbles with a large brush, roller, or squeegee.**

   Work from the center outward.

6. **Cut away the edges of your decoupage papers.**

7. **Allow the area to fully dry (one to two hours per coat).**

8. **Apply sealant on top.**

   Read Chapter 6 for information about working with sealant.

Gold Leaf

Gold leaf really brings the glamour! Applying gold leaf is an art known as *gilding*, and it's a technique that offers a ton of wow factor. Figure 5-7 shows a revamped chair that was gilded with gold leaf. (See the full transformation in Chapter 12.)

Gilding requires relatively few supplies:

>> **Gold leaf foil:** You can find this at craft stores. It's inexpensive because it's imitation gold made from a combination of brass, copper, and zinc.

>> **Water-based glue:** Size is the traditional glue used for gold leaf; however, other adhesives also work to varying degrees. (Size is an Old English word for glue.)

>> **Paintbrush:** You need a paintbrush to apply the size.

>> **Sealant:** Sealant is essential to protect the gold leaf.

Use the following steps to apply the gold leaf to your piece:

1. **Prepare your piece for gilding.**

   Clean, prep, prime, and paint your project according to your desired look. If you're gilding over bare wood, first give it a good clean and sand.

2. **Apply the gold size wherever you want the gold leaf to stick.**

TIP

   If you want a more worn gold leaf look, apply the size lightly. Dab your paintbrush into the size and then offload it onto a scrap piece of paper. Hold your paintbrush to the side and roll it over the tips or edges that you want to be detailed with gold. Figure 5-8 shows this technique of applying size.

3. **Allow the size to dry so that it's tacky to the touch.**

   This should take about 15 minutes.

FIGURE 5-7:
Judy Rom of
Upcycle
That made this
striking chair.

4. **Adorn with gold leaf.**

   Pick up the gold leaf by the protective tissue paper that it comes in. Put the shiny side directly onto the adhesive. Rub it in.

5. **Brush off the excess gold leaf.**

   You can save your scraps for another project.

6. **Distress with fine steel wool.**

   This is an optional step if you want your gold leaf to have a more aged look.

7. **Seal your piece to protect it from flaking off.**

FIGURE 5-8:
Hold the
paintbrush
horizontally to
roll it and apply
the size.

Chapter **6**

Finishing and Sealing Your Piece

After painting a piece to perfection, you need to seal in all that magic. Sealant is the best way to protect your upcycled furniture. The topcoat, or sealer, secures the paint and helps it adhere to the wood below. It also prevents your furniture from getting water damage, chips, and scratches. This step is especially important for high-traffic furniture like tables. The last thing you want is a water ring marring your beautiful paint job. Finishing your furniture with sealant keeps it looking fresh and fabulous for years to come.

The topcoat can have as much impact as the actual paint, and choosing the wrong kind can have disastrous effects. You don't want your beautiful white paint to turn yellow or that dark paint job to end up with a milky film.

In this chapter, you discover what sealant is and which kind to use for each project. I also explain the best techniques for using sealants, including working with a paintbrush, foam roller, paint sprayer, wax brush, or rag.

Getting to Know Sealants

Painted furniture without a topcoat is like a turtle without its shell. The sealant adds a hard finish that acts as a barrier between your furniture and the world. This protects your piece from scuffs and water damage, and it makes the surface of your upcycle easier to clean.

The three main categories of sealants are:

» Polyurethane

» Polycrylic

» Wax

TIP

Most sealants contain toxic volatile organic compounds (VOCs), if you want a food-safe sealant — for a painted wooden bowl or a cheese plate, for example — you can use hemp seed oil.

Table 6-1 gives you a breakdown of clear topcoats and when to use each one for finishing your furniture upcycles. Figure 6-1 shows an example of some good sealant options.

FIGURE 6-1:
Some sealants
that work well.

TABLE 6-1 **Sealant Best Use Guide**

Sealant Type	Formula	Ideal Use	Be Aware
Polyurethane	Oil-based	Great for a high-gloss finish and for heavy-traffic items exposed to lots of moisture and heat (e.g., wooden floors and outdoor furniture).	Oil-based polyurethane can dry with a yellowish tint. Contains a high level of VOCs, which are harmful gases that are emitted from the paint to the air. For safety, wear a mask when applying.
Polyurethane	Water-based	Highly resistant to scratches and water, so it's ideal for high-traffic interior furniture like cabinets and tables.	Looks cloudy when painted but dries clear. Depending on the brand, it can turn yellow when applied over white paint.
Polycrylic	Water-based finish that comes in brush-on and spray versions	The sealant of choice for most furniture upcycles because it's less smelly and toxic than polyurethane and it's easier to clean up. It also doesn't tend to turn yellow.	Polycrylics don't tolerate high heat as well as polyurethane does.
Furniture wax	Available in clear, white, dark, or metallic; dries to a matte finish and can be buffed to your desired sheen	Typically used over natural wood, chalk paint, or milk paint because it absorbs well into the porous surface and gives a nice, soft-looking sheen. It doesn't yellow on top of white paint. The darker waxes can create depth and detail.	Wax is water-resistant but not waterproof. You have to reapply it every six months.
Hemp seed oil	Food safe with a matte sheen	Works well over chalk and mineral-based paints. Looks great over black and brings out the luster of natural wood.	Cures in 21 days, after which it's water-resistant.

Using Sealants

Depending on the sealant you're using, you have a few different choices for application. You can use a paintbrush, foam roller, paint sprayer, wax brush, or rag.

Applying with a brush

If you want a high-gloss, durable finish, use an oil-based polyurethane. This sealant has a long working time before it starts drying, so you can use a high-quality synthetic brush to apply it. You can also use a brush to apply polycrylic; you just need to work a bit more quickly.

To figure out what size brush you need, think about the size of the piece you're using it for. A smaller brush gets into tight spots, whereas a bigger brush offers better coverage. A 2- to 3-inch angle brush is good for most projects, and it offers the best of both worlds. You can use the tapered brush tip for getting into corners.

Make sure to have the following materials on hand before you begin:

» Drop cloth

» Extra fine/high-grit sandpaper

» Tack cloth

» Stir stick

» Cup

» High-quality synthetic brush

» Oil-based polyurethane

» Mask

» Mineral spirits to clean oil-based poly off your brush

Use the following steps to apply sealant with a brush:

1. **Pick a well-ventilated area with plenty of fresh air and place a drop cloth under your piece to protect your floor from drips.**

   This is especially important for oil-based polyurethane because the chemicals in it make it super smelly and release toxic fumes. (Seriously, oil-based polyurethane *stinks*!)

   Protect yourself from the fumes by wearing a mask or respirator.

2. **Lightly sand your piece with extra-fine/high-grit sandpaper to get it smooth for finishing.**

3. **Use a tack cloth to remove all sanding dust.**

   You want to get your item as clean as possible before applying the topcoat; otherwise, you seal in any surface particles.

4. **Gently stir the poly until it has an even consistency.**

   You're a smooth operator, so never shake the can. Shaking causes air bubbles and can give your surface an uneven appearance. Use a stir stick instead.

5. **For the best results, pour some poly into a cup and then dip your brush there.**

   Don't dip your brush into the main poly pot because you can contaminate it with paint particles.

6. **Make sure you have poly on both sides of your brush and use long, even strokes, working in the same direction as the wood grain.**

TIP

Work in manageable sections of about 2 feet. Blend the sections while the poly is still wet by letting your brush gently glide along the surface. You want to apply a thin, even coat over the entire surface. The poly appears milky as you apply it, but it dries clear. Allow it to dry for at least 2 hours before applying a second coat.

7. **Lightly sand between coats to smooth out the surface and remove any paint drips and air bubbles.**

8. **Use a tack cloth to remove any sanding dust.**

9. **Repeat the topcoat painting process two more times.**

   Three coats is ideal coverage for a topcoat.

TIP

Place your brush in a sealed Ziploc bag between coats so it doesn't harden. When you're done working, you can clean the oil-based poly off your brush with mineral-based spirits.

Getting a flawless finish with a roller

If you use a water-based polyurethane or polycrylic, the working time is shorter than with an oil-based sealant because water-based varieties dry a lot faster. Because of this, you might want to use a foam roller when working on a large surface area like a tabletop.

Make sure to have the following materials on hand before you begin:

>> Drop cloth

>> Extra-fine/high-grit sandpaper

>> Damp lint-free cloth

>> Stir stick

>> Paint tray

>> High-density cabinet and door foam roller

>> Water-based polyurethane or polycrylic

>> Dish soap to clean the water-based sealant off your foam roller

Use the following steps to apply sealant with a foam roller:

1. **Set up a good painting environment with a drop cloth under your project.**

2. **Use an extra-fine/high-grit sandpaper to lightly sand your item to get it smooth and ready for finishing.**

TIP

3. **Wipe the piece down with a damp, lint-free cloth.**

   Oil and water don't mix well. You need to use a damp, lint-free cloth rather than an oil-based item like a tack cloth because you're using a water-based topcoat.

4. **Gently stir the poly with your stir stick.**

5. **Pour some poly into your painter's tray and then preload your roller with topcoat.**

6. **Roll it out in a long column.**

   If your surface has roller marks, you can go back over it with a 45-degree angle to get into all the grooves and fill in the gaps. After you've done that, lightly roll over it again to smooth it out. Figure 6-2 illustrates this technique.

7. **Gently roll between the overpasses to blend the areas.**

8. **Allow for the topcoat to dry completely (about 30 minutes to an hour) and then lightly sand between coats, remove the dusting grit, and then add another one-two topcoats.**

FIGURE 6-2: Shows the 45-degree angle used with a foam roller to eliminate roller marks.

Spraying sealant

Spray sealant is awesome because it gives a smooth and even finish with no brushstrokes. It's also handy for application because you can easily get into all the nooks and crannies.

Make sure to have the following materials on hand before you begin:

>> Drop cloth

>> Extra-fine/high-grit sandpaper

>> Tack cloth

>> Spray sealant

>> Mask

Use the following steps to apply spray sealant:

1. **Set up your work location in a well-ventilated area with a drop cloth under your piece.**

   Make sure the environment is between 65 and 85 degrees. This ensures good adhesion and a lovely, smooth texture on your finished piece.

2. **Lightly sand the surface using a fine-grit paper.**

   This gives your sealant something to stick to.

3. **Remove the sanding residue with a tack cloth.**

4. **Shake the can for a minute or two.**

5. **Put on your protective mask and spray with long and fluid spray strokes.**

   Keep the can vertical to prevent clogs and maintain a light pressure so that your coats are light.

TIP

   While in the midst of spraying, pause often to shake the can. Thin coats are better because they dry faster and help to avoid the wrinkled paint, which occurs when the paint is applied too thickly.

6. **Let the pieces fully dry.**

Working with wax

The original technique for sealing in chalk paint is with wax. Waxes come in clear, white, or dark. Clear wax seals and adds shine; white wax fills and highlights the wood grain; and dark wax brings depth to details and an aged, antique finish. Apply one or a combination.

Make sure to have the following materials on hand before you begin:

- » Furniture wax
- » Wax brush or rag
- » Lint-free cloth

Make sure the chalk paint is fully dry (at least a couple of hours of drying time) before you use the following steps to apply wax:

1. **Use a stiff bristled wax brush (or rag) and apply the furniture wax to the piece in large sections.**

   The wax slightly deepens the color, so you can see any spots you've missed by looking out for any paler bits.

2. **Brush the wax on and then wipe the excess off with a clean cloth.**

   Wax on, wax off, Karate Kid!

3. **Leave the piece overnight to dry and then buff it to your desired sheen.**

   The more you buff, the shinier the item gets.

4. **The wax will cure and harden over the coming weeks.**

   It takes at least a week for wax to become durable and resistant to water. Also, wax durability decreases over time. Consider rewaxing high-traffic pieces annually.

Applying oil

For a low-fi, food-safe solution, wipe on hemp seed oil with a rag.

Make sure to have the following materials on hand before you begin:

- » Hemp seed oil
- » Lint-free cloth

Use the following steps to wipe on hemp seed oil:

1. **Apply hemp oil to a lint-free cloth and wipe in circular motions.**

2. **Allow the hemp oil to penetrate over the next 12 hours.**

3. **Use a lint-free cloth to remove the excess oil and buff the item to your desired sheen.**

Hemp-oil takes two weeks to a month to cure, so be gentle with it in the meantime.

Chapter 7

Adding Patina and Final Touches to Make Your Piece Pop

Patina is the distressed surface that develops on furniture as a result of grime and time. It's the lustrous sheen of a beloved farmhouse table that's been worn through handling, telling a story that transports us through time and space. This natural aging contributes to an item's beauty, and is highly prized in the decor world.

This character is so desirable that it has inspired a whole style called *shabby chic*. The aesthetic is characterized by chippy paint, distressed edges, and weathered wood. It's all about creating the look of well-worn, antique furniture with peeka-boo flashes of previous layers.

In this chapter, I explain the techniques to distress furniture so you don't have to wait years to accomplish the look. I also share how to choose and install furniture hardware to complete your piece.

Putting on a Finish with Patina

Patina is the epitome of rustic charm. It's the perfectly imperfect finish of an item that's well used and loved. Once upon a time, this sort of look would have taken decades to acquire. Fortunately, you can now fake it (till you make it) with these fun techniques:

>> Distressing with sandpaper and tools

>> Aging wood with tea, vinegar, and steel wool

>> Whitewashing

>> Dry brushing

>> Creating layers with petroleum jelly

>> Scraping

>> Wet distressing

TIP

Mix and match a few techniques to get your desired patina. Figure 7-1 highlights how to transform the same board by using different techniques.

Table 7-1 compares the techniques and clarifies the best time to use each one.

FIGURE 7-1:
The original (untreated) board is on the top right. Going clockwise from there: antique tea and steel wool stain, whitewashing, paint applied with a scraper, wet distressing, scraping, petroleum jelly patina, and dry brushing.

TABLE 7-1   Patina Style Guide

Patina Technique	Design Look	Result	Ideal Use
Sandpaper	Rustic, shabby chic, antique look	Classic distressed look that works when you want to keep the original paint	Painted furniture that you want to age, or furniture that's already been scratched
Aging with vinegar, steel wool, and tea	Farmhouse, rustic, reclaimed, aged wood look	A natural way to give wood a soft and beautifully worn finish	Raw or unfinished wood
Whitewashing	Farmhouse, Scandinavian, modern	Brightens and showcases the wood grain; works well on smooth or textured wood	Walls, pallets, and reclaimed wood
Dry brushing	Rustic, beach house, farmhouse	A worn-in look	Textured wood like pallets or reclaimed wood; works best on a piece previously painted with a color you like or repainting with the base color and dry brushing on top with a second shade
Creating layers with petroleum jelly	Shabby chic, farmhouse	A "chippy paint" effect with multiple colors	Large furniture pieces crying out for more character
Scraping	Beach house, rustic, farmhouse	A gently weathered look	Flat pieces like the top or front of a dresser
Wet distressing	Antique, faded look, rustic, shabby chic	A classic result similar to sanding but without the mess	A great way to distress when you're working inside

REMEMBER

It's important to clean and prepare your furniture *before* you add patina so that you aren't working with a dirty, dusty piece, and so that the new paint adheres. See Chapter 4 for directions on how to do that.

Distressing with sandpaper and tools

A few dents and dings can add character to your piece. You can do basic distressing with sandpaper, steel wool, a nail, or a hammer. Essentially you're mimicking the look of furniture that's been scratched and bumped over time.

Figure 7-2 shows an example of a weathered bedside table.

AFTER

BEFORE

FIGURE 7-2:
A bedside table
that's been
weathered
with
sandpaper.

TIP

Sanding is a terrific way to remove some of the paint and add an authentic, distressed look. Focus on the edges and corners that stick out because they're the areas that would have naturally gotten worn with time and use.

Make sure you have the following materials on hand before you begin:

>> Fine-grit sandpaper, such as 220 grit

>> Sanding block (optional)

>> Tools like a hammer and nail, awl, metal chain, and wire brush

>> Scrap wood to test techniques (optional)

TIP

An awl is a small pointed tool that's primarily used for piercing holes in leather.

When you've gathered your materials, use one of the following methods or some combination of them:

>> Apply a light pressure and sand the edges of the furniture. You can always sand more, but you can't undo what's already been sanded off. Distress until you achieve your desired look.

>> Hit your piece with a hammer or metal chain to create divots in the wood. If you want an irregular pattern, fill a sock with nails and hammer over that.

>> To create an aged texture, scratch the wood with a nail, awl, or wire brush.

TIP

Reclaimed wood often has wormholes. (I'm not talking about a shortcut through space and time.) You can re-create this look by driving an awl into the wood.

TIP

Test out these distressing techniques on a scrap piece of wood to see how they look before committing your furniture.

Aging wood with tea, vinegar, and steel wool

Did you ever use tea to create "ye-olde" paper for elementary school projects? Try using tea and vinegar with steel wool to achieve a rustic, aged look for wood.

This fun technique feels a bit like a science experiment. The steel wool oxidizes from the acid of the vinegar, and when combined with tea it adds tannins, which turn the wood a darker color.

TIP

The effect of this method differs depending on what kind of wood the furniture is and the type of tea that you use. Test an inconspicuous patch of your piece before you go all-in on the technique.

Figure 7-3 shows the dramatic effect of this aging technique.

TIP

If the piece you're upcycling is painted, make sure to sand off the paint first; otherwise, this solution doesn't take.

Gather what you need to age wood with tea and steel wool:

>> White vinegar

>> Superfine steel wool, grade 0000 (also referred to as 4/0); *do not* use pre-soaped steel wool pads

>> Two black tea bags for every cup of water

   If you want, you can experiment with various kinds of tea. The darker the tea, the darker the stain.

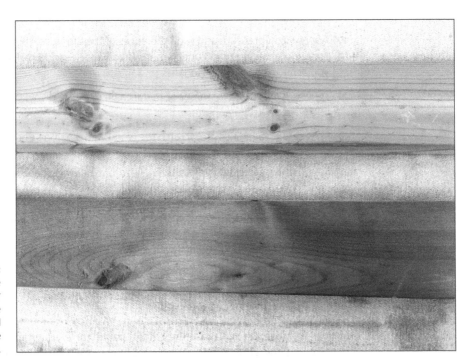

FIGURE 7-3:
The before
(top) and after
(below) of the
steel wool and
tea technique
on pine.

>> Two glass jars

>> Hot water

>> Rags or a paintbrush

>> Gloves

>> Sealant

Then follow these steps:

1. **Pour the vinegar into a jar; then pull apart the steel wool and submerge it into the vinegar.**

   Leave the jar *uncovered* for 10–24 hours. This detail is important because the oxidization process produces gas. The steel wool starts to dissolve in the vinegar. The longer you leave the steel wool, the darker the vinegar becomes.

2. **Clean and sand your piece so that it's ready to receive the solution.**

3. **In another jar, steep the tea bags with hot water.**

   Steep the tea bags anywhere from 15 minutes to 12 hours. The longer they steep, the darker your result. Allow the tea to cool to room temperature before you use it.

4. **Wipe or brush the tea onto the wood and let it dry completely.**

5. **Apply the vinegar/steel wool solution and let it dry for a minimum of 24 hours.**

6. **Protect the finish by sealing it. See Chapter 6 for these techniques.**

TIP

The wood continues to age as it dries, so let it dry completely before deciding if you want to add a second coat.

REMEMBER

Work in a well-ventilated space and leave your steel wool/vinegar jar uncovered. The hydrogen gas produced during the process needs an avenue to safely release.

Whitewashing

Whitewashing or limewashing is a throwback technique often used in farmhouse style. Traditionally, farmhouses were whitewashed using lime from limestone, water, and salt. Other ingredients like molasses, pine resin, tallow oils, and milk solids were often added to make it more waterproof. This treatment brightened the farm buildings, slowed their deterioration, and made them antifungal and fire retardant. These days whitewashing is a lot simpler. You use diluted white paint!

Figure 7-4 shows an example of a whitewashed wall.

FIGURE 7-4: A lovely example of a wall painted with the whitewashing technique.

Whitewashing is a great way to showcase natural wood grains. When you whitewash, the paint looks a bit translucent, meaning you get to see the wood grains underneath. This is different from painting a pure, opaque white, which covers the details of the wood completely.

Here's what you need to whitewash:

>> Water-based and nontoxic paint, such as chalk paint, acrylic, or latex

>> Water

>> Mixing cup

>> Lint-free rag or tack cloth

>> Medium grit sandpaper like 120 grit

Follow these steps to apply the whitewash effect:

1. **Sand the wood and clean off the sanding grit with the tack cloth.**

2. **In your mixing cup, dilute the white paint with water until it's the consistency of crêpe batter.**

3. **Dip the lint-free rag into the diluted paint and then spread it across the wood in the same direction as the wood grain.**

4. **Allow the paint to dry.**

   You can use as many layers as you want to achieve your desired opacity.

You can also use this technique with colored paint instead of white. You guessed it — then it's called color washing!

If you want a patchier finish that looks more like rustic barnwood, don't dilute the paint. Pour it on and spread it with a paint scraper instead of a rag. This technique works best on reclaimed wood boards that have a lot of texture.

Figure 7-5 shows examples of a board whitewashed with a rag and another done with a scraper.

Dry brushing

The dry brush technique has a characteristic scratchy look. It's done with a relatively dry paintbrush, hence the name.

Figure 7-6 shows an example of a piece of furniture that's been dry brushed with blue paint.

FIGURE 7-5:
The board whitewashed with a rag is on the top, and the one done with a scraper is on the bottom.

FIGURE 7-6:
The dry brush technique is shown here.

The key to this technique is to touch your brush *very lightly* to the wood. It should barely touch it, like a sweet hint of a caress.

Here's what you need to dry brush:

>> A paintbrush

>> Paint

>> Paint palette or plate

>> Damp rag

>> Shop towels (heavy-duty paper towels that won't disintegrate)

Follow these steps to apply the dry brush technique:

1. **Dip your brush tip into paint and then skim most of it off on the edge of the can or paint palette; then wipe even more onto a drop cloth or paper towel.**

2. **Using a light and quick hand, start at the edge of the piece and brush straight in the direction of the grain.**

   For larger pieces, you can use an X pattern for more texture. Either way, your paintbrush should barely kiss the surface of the wood.

3. **When no more paint is coming off your brush, reload the brush using the same dip and offload method.**

4. **It's up to your personal preference how many layers and colors to add.**

You can use two or more colors with this technique. If you want more dimensions, layer on additional colors using the same dry brush technique.

If you're too heavy-handed with the brush or paint, you'll end up with unnatural-looking streaks. If this happens, you can either remove the paint immediately with a damp cloth or wait for it to dry and then layer more colors on top.

Creating layers with petroleum jelly

This technique is brilliant for creating an awesome, chippy paint look, without the mess of sanding. It allows you to overlap colors in a beautiful shabby chic style. In the areas you add petroleum jelly, the paint doesn't stick, and the color underneath peeks through.

Figure 7-7 shows an example of wood that's been painted with this style.

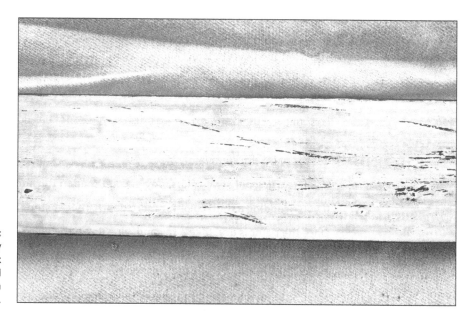

TIP

Think about the color scheme you want before you start. The first color you paint is revealed after you remove the petroleum jelly, and the last color you paint has the most coverage on top. You can layer one, two, three, or more colors.

Gather these supplies:

>> Petroleum jelly

>> A foam brush

>> An inexpensive paintbrush

>> Rags or shop towels

>> Multiple paint colors

>> Wax or hemp oil

Apply the petroleum jelly technique with these steps:

1. **Look at your piece and decide what areas you want to make the most distressed.**

   Generally, distressed areas are the places that get rubbed and worn, like edges, doors, corners, and legs.

2. **Paint your base coat and allow it to dry completely.**

   You don't need to worry about getting perfect full coverage because you'll put more layers of paint on top of this base coat.

3. **Dip your foam brush into the petroleum jelly and dab it onto the areas you want the paint to look chippy.**

4. **Imagine that the petroleum jelly isn't there and paint a different color on top.**

   I recommend using an inexpensive brush so you don't gunk up your good brushes.

5. **Let the paint dry completely.**

6. **If you're using only two colors, do a second coat on top and let it fully dry.**

7. **If you're adding a third color for more depth, repeat steps 3 through 6.**

8. **Once the paint is dry, take a rag and wipe down the piece.**

   This is the fun part! The petroleum jelly wipes off and reveals the gorgeous, chippy layers beneath!

9. **Make sure all the petroleum jelly is fully removed, and then finish your piece with wax or hemp oil (as opposed to a water-based sealant) to seal in the look.**

TIP

You can also incorporate the piece's original finish as a chippy layer. To do this, skip painting a base color (step 2) and put petroleum jelly directly on the areas you want to shine through as chippy paint.

TIP

An alternative option (with a similar look) is using a beeswax bar or a candle instead of petroleum jelly. Rub it *hard* on the places you don't want the paint to adhere, and follow the rest of the preceding steps.

Scraping

Scraping is similar to sanding except that you remove some paint with a paint scraper before the paint has completely dried. The effect is faded, worn, and weathered, like wood at a beach house.

Figure 7-8 shows an example of wood that's been fatigued by scraping.

Have the following items on hand for scraping:

» Paint

» Paintbrush

FIGURE 7-8:
The scraping
technique is
shown here.

>> Paint scraper or cabinet scraper

>> Damp rag

When you're ready to go, use these steps:

1. **Paint the wood and let it partially dry so that it still feels a bit tacky to the touch.**

2. **Working in the same direction as the wood grain, scrape off some of the paint with a scraper.**

Make sure to scrape the paint flecks off your piece; otherwise, they can get stuck in the drying paint.

TIP

Wet distressing

Did I save the best for last? Maybe. Wet distressing is one of the easiest and most effective ways to create natural-looking aging. In a nutshell, you paint a layer of paint, let it dry partially, and then wipe off some paint from grooves and edges.

Figure 7-9 shows an example of a board that's been wet distressed.

FIGURE 7-9:
Here's an
example of the
wet distress
technique.

Here's what you need for wet distressing:

>> Paint

>> Paintbrush

>> Lint-free cloth

>> Bucket of water

>> Scouring pad (optional)

Take the following steps to give your furniture the wet distressed look:

1. **Paint your furniture and allow it to partially dry for about 20 minutes.**

2. **Wet your cloth and wring it out. Then apply light pressure to rub paint away from the corners and natural wear spots, or wherever you want to reveal the original finish.**

TIP

Start rubbing with a gentle pressure so you don't take off too much paint too quickly. You can always increase your pressure as necessary.

It can help to mist the item with a spray bottle of water before wiping. If the paint has dried for too long, you can use a scouring pad instead of a rag.

TIP

3. **Wet distress away until you're happy with the look.**

Making Pieces Functional with Furniture Hardware

Hardware is like the cherry on top of your upcycle. This section discusses the most important factors for selection, and how to install it.

Choosing hardware

Hardware is the ultimate furniture accessory. When it comes to choosing, keep these factors in mind:

» Types of hardware — knobs or pulls

» Style

» Finish

» Size

Knobs or pulls

Knobs are smaller and are installed with a single screw. Pulls are longer and are installed with two screws. Generally, cabinets and doors get knobs and drawers get pulls, but there's no rule that says you *have* to do it that way. For instance, you might like the look of a pull placed vertically on a cabinet.

The type of hardware you choose has a lot to do with your personal preference. There's no right or wrong choice. You can even experiment with making upcycled drawer pulls from secondhand leather belts!

Figure 7-10 shows one entertainment console with all knobs, one with all pulls, and one with both.

It's easier to open drawers that have pulls because they offer more grip. This is an important consideration for heavy drawers.

Knobs are generally less expensive than pulls. They're also easier to install because they have just one screw.

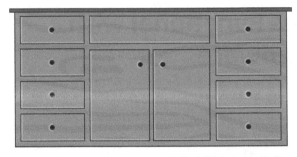

ALL KNOBS

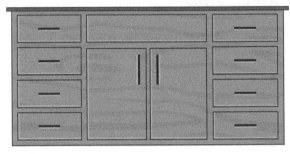

ALL PULLS

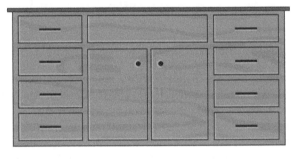

KNOBS + PULLS

FIGURE 7-10:
Different
styles of
hardware
on an
entertainment
center.

Style

The style of hardware you choose should reflect the design of your piece and its intended home. For example, a sleek, linear pull might be at odds with a rustic, aged piece in a farmhouse kitchen.

TIP

For a cohesive look, select a style similar to the design of your piece.

Material and finish

Most hardware is made of a metal alloy such as stainless steel, pewter, brass, or bronze; however, there are also beautiful options that are ceramic, glass, enamel, or crystal. There are lots of options for the finish — polished, matte, weathered, oil-rubbed, and painted are just a few.

TIP

Generally speaking, warm paint tones and rustic pieces look great with gold, bronze, or black hardware. Silver and black look great with cold tones and more contemporary or white pieces.

Size

When it comes to choosing the size of the hardware, functionality comes first. The hardware should be big enough to do what it needs to do without overpowering the piece.

Figure 7-11 shows suggestions for the size of hardware to drawer or cabinet.

TIP

In general, a pull should be one-third the length of the cabinet or drawer it'll be on.

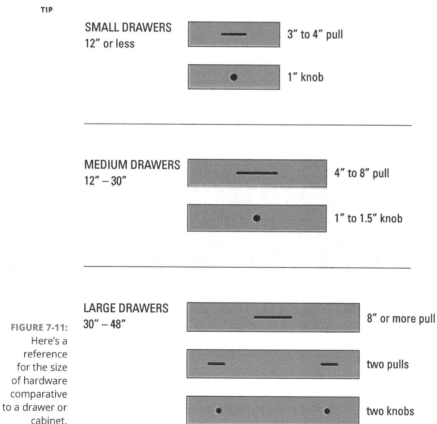

FIGURE 7-11: Here's a reference for the size of hardware comparative to a drawer or cabinet.

SMALL DRAWERS
12" or less

3" to 4" pull

1" knob

MEDIUM DRAWERS
12" – 30"

4" to 8" pull

1" to 1.5" knob

LARGE DRAWERS
30" – 48"

8" or more pull

two pulls

two knobs

The hardware you choose should feel good. Test how it feels in your hand and hold it up to your piece to see how it looks before you install it.

Installing hardware

It's easy to install hardware. You can attach knobs with a screwdriver and a screw or by hand with a nut and a washer. Slide the knob through the hole at the front of the drawer or door and secure it in place with the screw or washer and bolt that it comes with.

Figure 7-12 shows how a knob secured with a washer and bolt should look.

FIGURE 7-12:
An installed knob has the washer and bolt flush with the backside of the drawer.

Perhaps the piece originally had a knob, and you want to switch it to a pull. To do this you need the following supplies:

>> Ruler

>> Pencil

>> Cabinet hardware installation template (optional)

>> Wood putty

>> Putty knife

» Fine-grit sandpaper

» Screwdriver with drill bit

Here's how to do it:

1. **Measure the distance between the two screws on the pull.**

   This measurement is called the spread.

2. **Place the pull over the original hole and mark with a pencil where the two new holes will be.**

   Use a ruler or a cabinet hardware installation template to make sure the new holes are evenly spaced on either side of the original hole. Figure 7-13 highlights the positioning of this.

FIGURE 7-13:
Shows how to measure the spread of the drawer pull.

3. **Using a putty knife or your finger, fill in the original hole with wood putty and wipe off the excess; then let it dry completely.**

4. **Sand the area smooth with fine-grit sandpaper and touch it up with paint if necessary.**

5. **With a screwdriver, drill pilot holes into the pencil marks.**

6. **Line up the new hardware and slip it into the pilot holes; then secure the screw from the back with a screwdriver.**

TIP

To figure out what size drill bit you need for the pilot holes, look at the size of the body of the screw, not including the threads. If you size too wide, the screw will be loose in the hole. It's better to start smaller and size up if necessary.

Chapter **8**

Rejuvenating Antiques

Furniture restoration is a fantastic way to bring old pieces back to life. It's like a Scandinavian spa — but for furniture. The piece transforms from shabby and unkempt to gleaming and renewed.

Vintage furniture — well-built, sturdy, solid-wood furniture — deserves a second chance. This furniture is high quality, especially compared to the soul less "fast furniture" being pumped out today. Unfortunately, they don't make 'em like they used to.

Fret not, there are still gems to be found. Scoop them up at your local thrift stores, garage sales, and from family and friends. Done correctly, furniture restoration increases the beauty, value, and desirability of the piece. This is your opportunity to snag fine wine for the price of grape juice.

In this chapter, I explain what furniture restoration is and how to do it. You can dive into a hands-on, step-by-step guide to refinishing a dining room chair. Get ready for the glow up!

Understanding What Furniture Restoration Is

So, you've found a beautiful old piece of furniture and you're thinking about restoring or refinishing it. Great!

Although the terms are often used interchangeably, there's technically a difference between furniture *restoration* and *refinishing*. In a nutshell, furniture *restoration* is all about returning the piece to its former glory and look. On the other hand, furniture *refinishing* implies removing and replacing the current finish.

Depending on the piece, the restoration process can be as simple as a thorough cleaning or as complex as replacing rare parts and hand-carved appliques (see Figure 8-1). When done properly, furniture restoration maintains and increases the value of the item. That's why true furniture restoration is generally used for antiques and collectibles.

FIGURE 8-1:
Hand-carved appliques can be challenging to replace.

TIP

The key to restoring is to do as little as possible to revive the original look of the piece. Take the path of least resistance. This might mean just a good clean and polish.

Refinishing involves stripping and sanding the piece down to the bones and then building 'er back up again. The piece is reborn. Figure 8-2 shows the results of the refinishing steps I go through later on in this chapter.

FIGURE 8-2:
Furniture
refinishing
offers amazing
results!

Restoring and Repairing

Vintage solid-wood pieces that are 50–99 years old are ideal for restoring. These items are well made and feature quality artisanship that's worth preserving.

But before you do any restoration or refinishing, you need to determine whether the piece you've found is worth saving. The main factors to consider are:

>> **Dovetail joints:** A strong joinery technique of interlocking "pins" and "tails". Refer to Chapter 2 to see an image of a dovetail joint.

>> **Sturdy build:** Solid wood and good bones are ideal.

>> **Manufacturer's stamps:** A stamp is a sign of high quality that has been placed on the furniture by an artisan. A newer, factory-made piece won't have a maker's mark). Figure 8-3 shows a stamp on the piece.

TIP

Do the "rickety test" and shake the piece back and forth to see how solid it is. You want a piece that's structurally sound.

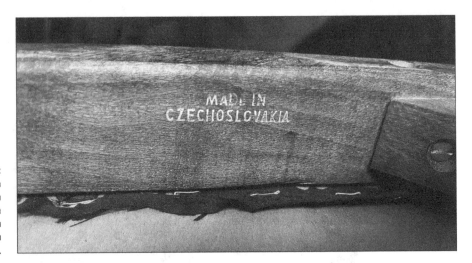

FIGURE 8-3:
The stamp on the bottom indicates a quality item made by an artisan.

Getting started

As with any project, you should make sure you have the supplies you need for the various stages of furniture restoring. These are the materials you'll use:

>> **Cleaning:** Dish soap, warm water, buckets and bowls, clean rags and cloths, old toothbrush, mineral spirits, vacuum

>> **Stripping:** Sandpaper (various grits), electric sander, sanding block, chemical stripper, putty knife

>> **Repairing:** Epoxy putty, wood restorer, wood filler, wood glue, antique wax, oxalic acid, an iron, stir sticks, clamps

>> **Painting:** Paint, stain, paintbrushes, drop cloth

>> **Sealant:** Wood sealant, wax, poly

>> **Safety:** Goggles, mask, gloves

REMEMBER

Every restoration starts with a solid cleaning. Vacuum the piece and then give it a proper scrub with a mix of dish soap and warm water. Old toothbrushes are great for getting into the nooks and crannies.

When the piece is good and clean, assess the finish to determine your next steps. Wipe the piece with mineral spirits to temporarily reveal how it would look with clear finish. This won't harm the piece, and you might discover that all it needs is a good coating of sealant.

Here are some signs that you need to further restore the piece:

>> Water rings and blemishes are visible.

>> The finish is peeling and flaking.

>> Even after cleaning, the surface is sticky.

>> Wood cracks are present.

Removing the old finish

You can strip the finish off the wood in three ways:

>> Scraping with a paint scraper if the finish is flaky

>> Sanding with sandpaper if the finish has a light sheen

>> Stripping with a chemical stripper if the finish is very glossy

If you need to scrape, follow these steps:

1. **Scrape off the brittle finish with a paint scraper or putty knife.**

2. **Sand any remaining bits of finish with fine-grit sandpaper.**

To use sanding as your stripping method, follow these steps:

1. **Start sanding with a medium-grit sandpaper.**

   Sand until most of the finish is off.

2. **Switch to a fine-grit to remove the last bits of the former finish.**

Using a chemical stripper is a little more involved than the other two methods. Here's what you need to do:

1. **Set up your work area in a well-ventilated space. Wear gloves, a mask, and eye protection.**

2. **Apply chemical stripper with a disposable brush.**

3. **Allow the stripper time to work its magic.**

4. **Scrape off the old finish with a putty knife.**

5. **Use mineral spirits and steel wool to clean off the residue of the previous finish.**

Removing black marks

Oxalic acid is brilliant for removing black stains from wood that has been exposed to metals and moisture. Use the following steps to apply oxalic acid to remove the black marks:

1. **Buy oxalic acid in crystal form from an online retailer.**

2. **Dissolve the oxalic acid in hot water according to the manufacturer's directions.**

3. **While wearing heavy-duty gloves and a mask, dip a rag into the mixture and wipe the whole wooden panel, not just the stained area.**

   Wiping the full area ensures that the color removal is consistent across the whole surface.

4. **Let the wood dry fully.**

5. **Assess whether the stain was fully removed or if it needs another application.**

   Repeat steps 3 and 4 if needed until the stain has disappeared.

6. **Add baking soda to water and wash off the crystals to neutralize the acid.**

   The basic baking soda neutralizes the acidic oxalic acid.

7. **Allow the furniture to dry fully before sealing.**

WARNING

Be aware that you're handling an acid. Wear protection. Don't brush the crystals into the air or onto the ground because doing so will cause you to cough. And never mix the oxalic acid with another chemical or bleach.

Removing white rings

White rings on furniture come from moisture that has soaked into the wood sealant and gotten trapped. Figure 8-4 shows the dreaded water rings.

Water rings aren't a total deal breaker. Here are a few different methods for removing them:

>> **An iron:** Place a t-shirt over the stain and then iron over it on a low setting. *Avoid using the steam function* as this will make the stain worse. Try doing a spot test first. Check progress frequently.

>> **A hair dryer:** Move the hair dryer side to side on a low setting over the affected area.

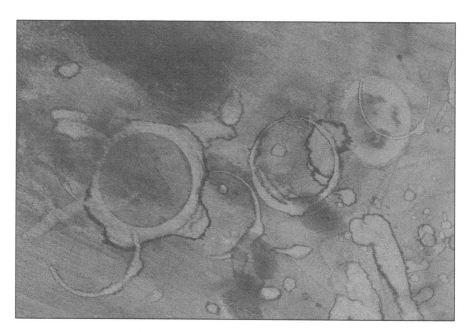

FIGURE 8-4:
Water rings
in wood.

>> **An equal mixture of olive oil and white vinegar:** Brush this mixture onto the wood in the direction of the grain. Wipe the whole surface of the wood. Follow by wiping with a clean, dry cloth.

>> **Mayonnaise or petroleum jelly:** Dab the mayonnaise or petroleum jelly onto the damaged area and allow it to sit for a few hours. Wipe it away with a clean, dry cloth.

Repairing scratches, chips, and cracks

To remove scratches, lightly sand with fine-grit sandpaper *in the direction of the wood grain.* Smooth out the area by sanding once again with extra-fine sandpaper. Clean off the dust and refinish the wood with oil or wax.

Wood putty is perfect for repairing smaller cracks and chips in wood. Use epoxy putty for larger gaps. This is the process for filling chips, and cracks:

1. Look for wood putty in the same shade as your wood.
2. Dab the putty on the crack using a putty knife.
3. Smooth the putty with the putty knife.
4. Let it dry fully.
5. Sand the area with fine-grit sandpaper to smooth it out.

If there are cracks in the wood, fill it with wood glue. In order to get the wood glue in, insert a toothpick into the split to carefully prop it open and then apply wood glue to the area with a stir stick. Then remove the toothpick and use paint tape or clamps to hold the area together while it dries.

Restoring missing color

There are a couple options for recoloring your furniture piece. You can use gel stain or wood stain.

Gel stain

Gel stain is wonderful for restoring furniture color. It's a bit of a miracle product, honestly, because you don't even have to strip the finish first. You can apply gel stain by following these steps:

1. **Wipe on the gel stain with a lint-free cloth.**
2. **Wipe with a clean, dry cloth to remove the excess stain.**
3. **Let it dry overnight.**
4. **Seal it with finish.**

    See Chapter 6.

TIP

If you don't like the result of the gel stain, you can use mineral spirits to wipe it away before it dries.

Wood stain

Wood stain is nice and easy to apply. You simply wipe it on as described here:

1. **Sand the piece down.**
2. **Use a tack cloth to remove the sanding dust.**
3. **Stir the wood stain and apply it with a clean, dry rag.**
4. **Wipe the area with a clean rag to remove the excess stain.**
5. **Add more layers as necessary.**
6. **Finish with sealant.**

    See Chapter 6.

TIP

It's hard to remove stain once it's on (unless you sand it down again), so it's best to start with light layers and build up to your desired color.

Refinishing Antique Furniture

Sometimes hands-on experience is the best teacher. If you want to follow along with the process step by step, here's an example of how to refinish a vintage dining room chair:

1. **Find a piece to refinish.**

   I found a vintage chair at a thrift shop. With its solid wood construction and a Made in Czechoslovakia stamp on the underside, this piece had great bones, but it was definitely ready for some TLC.

2. **Clean the piece.**

   After a solid cleaning, it was evident that this chair had significant water damage. Figure 8-5 shows the condition of the piece.

FIGURE 8-5:
Cleaning revealed the water damage.

3. **Sand the flaws away.**

   Based on my assessment, it seemed most effective to sand the piece down to remove the damage. For a job like this, start with a medium-grit sandpaper and work down to a fine grit.

4. Clean up the dust.

A tack cloth is perfect for removing the sanding dust so the debris doesn't get stuck in your new finish. Figure 8-6 shows the tack cloth in action.

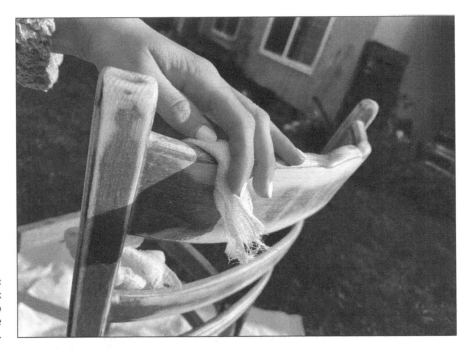

FIGURE 8-6: Using a tack cloth to remove the sanding dust.

5. Stain the wood.

Pick a stain that matches the color of the wood. Wipe it on with a clean, dry cloth. Start with a light coat and build up to your desired color. Figure 8-7 shows the staining process.

6. After the stain has dried, give it a light hand sand with a fine-grit sandpaper to smooth the piece and prepare it for finishing.

Seal in all that magic with a finish of your choice. I used wipe-on poly here. Figure 8-8 shows the finished frame stained, sealed and fabulous.

FIGURE 8-7:
Staining the
wood brings
it back to its
former glory,
sans the
damage.

FIGURE 8-8:
Glorious and
gleaming, the
chair is sanded,
stained, and
sealed.

7. **Finish to perfection.**

Reassemble your piece and add the finishing touches. In this case, I reupholstered the seat. Find out how to do that in Chapter 9. Figure 8-9 shows the final result.

FIGURE 8-9:
This chair is
refinished
and refreshed!

3

Other Upcycling Techniques

Learn the tools of the upholstery trade. Find out how to select a good piece and then strip, measure, staple, and trim your way to a crisp, new look.

Explore the options for upcycling glass bottles, including the techniques for cutting and drilling holes into glass.

Find out how to pick a good pallet, disassemble it, and get inspired to turn it into something fresh.

Find out the top tips for salvaging and reusing wood.

Chapter **9**

Upholstery 101

These days, most furniture is mass-produced and doesn't last five years. It wasn't always that way, though. Furniture used to be built by hand from real wood. Antique furniture was made with exquisite artisanship, and it was built to last.

Simply put, vintage is valuable. Older furniture was made with solid construction techniques and wood, which is a sharp contrast to the cheap, veneer-covered particleboard that's often used today. The great news is that a lot of that furniture is still around, and you can often find it secondhand for a song.

However, "good bones" aside, old furniture often comes with sad and outdated upholstery. But *by reupholstering*, you can switch out those raggedy patterns to give it a new lease on life. Reupholstering is the ideal way to revitalize old and outdated furniture.

Welcome to Upholstery 101! In this chapter, I explain what makes a piece worth reupholstering and how to go about it. You'll discover the tools of the trade and how to select fabric for your project. Finally, I delve into the process of reupholstering a dining room chair, which you can do it too by following the steps.

Considering Reupholstery

Reupholstering is exhilarating! With basic upholstery skills and a bit of TLC, you can give that settee a second lease on life. It feels a bit like waving a fairy god-mother wand and bibbiti-bobbiti-booing that old furniture into a fresh new 'fit.

Here are some scenarios that bode well for reupholstering:

>> **It's a sentimental piece.** Perhaps it's something that's been in your family for a while.

>> **The item is valuable.** It features solid hardwood and incredible "bones," aka the wooden frame of the piece.

>> **The craftwork is superb.** It's a vintage or antique piece made with traditional techniques and is built to last a lifetime.

>> **It would work well in your space.** The style and size of the piece are a perfect fit.

>> **You value solid, well-made furniture built to last.** Reupholstering is a big, green step away from disposable, fast furniture.

TIP

Items with a maker's mark or those that say they were made in a European country are good indicators of high quality from a vintage era.

Selecting a good piece

You thrift a good chair for an awesome price and imagine it would look perfect . . . if only the fabric were different. Now you're wondering if it's worth reupholstering. Well, is it? Not all furniture you find is worth saving.

Some items are worth reupholstering, and some, quite frankly, aren't worth the cost and time. That's why it's important to carefully consider items before committing to them.

Here are a few situations in which reupholstery doesn't make sense:

>> The piece feels rocky and uneven.

>> The springs feel wacky when you press on them or sit on the piece.

>> The foam feels crackly and petrified.

>> You see bugs or signs of bugs (droppings, shedding, fecal matter).

When choosing pieces to reupholster, look for high-quality furniture that's solid. Ideally, only the fabric should need replacing. Take a look at the underside of the piece to scope the frame's condition. You might have to lift up the dust cover (the underside fabric of the piece) to see.

Start small. Pieces with simple construction, where fabric can be stapled on (like a dining chair), are perfect for beginners.

Learning the tools of the trade

The basic tools you need for upholstery are:

>> Staple gun

>> Upholstery staples (⅜" or ½")

>> Forked staple remover or flat-head screwdriver

>> Fabric scissors

>> Measuring tape

>> Chalk for marking fabric

>> Spray adhesive or white glue

The following items are nice to have:

>> Work gloves

>> Ground sheet/tarp to contain staples

>> Needle-nose pliers

>> Hammer

>> A sharp knife or handsaw for cutting foam

Your project materials will vary based on the piece but will likely include these:

>> Fresh fabric for upholstering

>> New foam (depending on the condition of the current foam)

>> Dacron or polyester batting — sometimes you don't need to replace the current foam and can add a bit of batting for extra padding instead

Choosing the best fabric

Upholstery fabrics come in two main types: natural and synthetic. Natural fabric is plant or animal based; examples are cotton, wool, silk, leather, and linen. Synthetic fibers are human-made and include polyester, acrylic, nylon, viscose, acetate, and vinyl.

Table 9-1 highlights the pros and cons of various upholstery fabrics.

TABLE 9-1   **Upholstery Fabric Best Use Guide**

Fabric Type	Composition	Pros	Cons
Cotton	Natural	Comes in a huge range of colors. Soft and breathable fabric. Removeable covers are easy to wash.	Likely to stain. Lacks elasticity and is susceptible to fading and tears.
Linen	Natural	Feels soft and stylish. Easy to clean. Eco-friendly. Softens over time.	Absorbs stains. Wrinkles easily and isn't very durable because it's a thin material.
Silk	Natural	Soft and regal feeling. A strong natural fabric that retains its shape over time.	Expensive. Will break down in direct sunlight.
Velvet	Natural or synthetic	Soft and sumptuous. Can be vacuumed to clean. Durable; will last for a long time if treated with care.	Attracts dust and pet hair. Fades under direct sunlight. Not machine washable.
Wool	Natural	Soft and cozy. Naturally resistant to mold and fire.	Hot for summer and warmer climates. A more expensive fabric. Must be dry cleaned.
Vinyl	Synthetic	Very durable and requires little maintenance. Easy to wipe with a cloth to clean. Highly affordable.	Less luxurious than leather. Not breathable. Susceptible to cracking, which is very noticeable and hard to repair without replacing the full fabric.
Leather	Natural	Classic luxurious look. Ages well. Highly resistant to wear and tear. Low maintenance; can be wiped to clean.	Can be expensive. Not ideal when the weather is too hot or cold because it can feel sticky against bare skin, or cold to the touch if the room is cool.
Polyester	Synthetic	Soft and durable. Comes in a wide variety of designs and colors. Easy to clean.	Not very eco-friendly. Can be flammable.

Fabric Type	Composition	Pros	Cons
Olefin	Synthetic	Looks and feels like wool but is less pricey. Durable and low-maintenance. Stain resistant. Can be used outdoors.	Susceptible to damage from heat and light. Doesn't have much color variety.
Sunbrella	Synthetic	Resists sun fade. Ideal for outdoor use.	Expensive. Doesn't feel soft to the touch. Not eco-friendly.

The factor used for measuring fabric durability is called the double rub count. It's a testing method in which a machine goes back and forth over a fabric to see how many "double rubs" it can withstand. The double rub count is broken into two grade categories:

>> **Residential grades are 3,000–25,000 double rubs.** These fabrics are cheaper and will last about 1–3 years.

>> **Commercial grades are 40,000–100,000+ double rubs.** These fabrics are made to be extremely resilient and will last for 10–20 years.

Here's what you should consider when selecting fabric:

>> Look and feel

>> Alignment with your lifestyle

>> Durability and resilience to sunlight, soil, and abrasion

>> Maintenance, care, and stain-proofing

When choosing a fabric, consider the purpose of the furniture piece. If it's going to be a high-use, family item, it makes more sense to go with something more durable and easier to clean.

TIP

Solid colors are more forgiving than patterns when you first start reupholstering. Patterns, especially lines, will go wonky if you pull one corner more tightly than the others.

TIP

Upcycling your fabric is an option. Vintage bedding, curtains, and silk scarves are fabulous options for fabric. Keep an eye on the textile aisle at your local thrift store to see what's available.

Reupholstering a Chair

For your first foray into reupholstering, it's great to start with a piece that has easily removable seating, like a dining chair.

Stripping to prepare for something fresh

The first step to reupholstery is the teardown. It involves taking apart the furniture to the point where you can remove the old fabric.

Take pics of items during teardown so you have a reference of what goes where. You might need those "before" pictures later!

Teardown for a dining room chair means removing the seat from the chair. Sometimes the seat is simply sitting in a "frame," and you can pop it up from the bottom; other times it's screwed into the chair frame. Figure 9-1 shows how you can turn the chair upside down to remove the screws.

When the seat is separate, take a solid look at how the corners were done. Having pics to reference later can be helpful, so snap some more photos!

FIGURE 9-1: Remove the screws to separate the seat from the chair.

Figure 9-2 shows how the previous corners were done.

FIGURE 9-2:
It's helpful to
see how the
corners were
stapled the last
time around.

To remove the old fabric, a forked staple remover is helpful. If you don't have one, you can use a flat-head screwdriver or needle-nose pliers. Figure 9-3 shows how to remove staples with a screwdriver.

TIP

When you have removed the old fabric, suss out the condition of the foam and wood to see whether it's reusable or needs to be replaced.

Measuring and cutting foam

If you need to replace the foam, use the plywood base of the chair as a template. Glue the plywood on top of a piece of foam that's larger than the wood; then cut off the excess foam with a sharp knife or saw.

TIP

Sometimes the old foam is reusable, but you want to add more padding. In this case, glue the old foam and base on top of the new foam. Then cut off the excess foam around the sides.

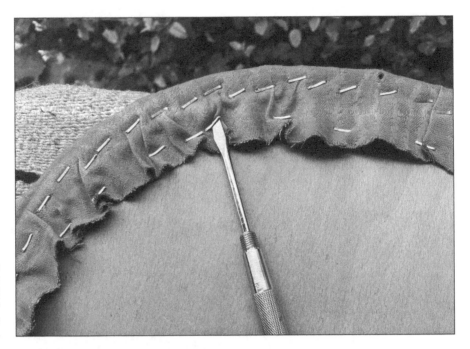

FIGURE 9-3:
Using a
flat-head
screwdriver
to remove
staples.

TIP

If you can, ask to have your foam cut to size when you purchase it from a foam or upholstery shop. Bring the old base with you and politely inquire whether the store can do it. It will save you a *bunch* of time.

Fabric measurements and cutting

Here's how to measure and cut your fabric:

1. **Take the measurements of the piece.**

   Measure the widest part from front to back and side to side. Also measure and include the height of the foam and a few extra inches to each measurement (4") for wrapping and stapling.

2. **Lay the fabric on a table and line it up with the edges so that your fabric is square and even.**

3. **Measure out your required dimensions and mark the fabric accordingly with chalk.**

4. **Cut out the fabric using fabric scissors.**

TIP

Label the top or front of your cut fabric so you know where it's going.

Another option for measuring fabric is to use the teardown as a pattern. When you remove the previous fabric, you can use it as a template. Remember to add a few extra inches to accommodate for new foam.

Stapling your way to a new look

Lay out your fabric panel and match the front with the front of your chair base. Now staple in a "temporary", which is a temporarily placed staple that will help hold the fabric in place for pulling.

Now do the same to the sides. You'll end up with four temporaries — one on each side. Figure 9-4 shows what this looks like.

FIGURE 9-4: Temporaries on each side.

It's time to start stapling for real. Here's how:

1. **Working from the back, make the fabric tight and smooth by tugging the fabric taut and pulling it forward and up and over the edge of the foam and fabric with your hand.**

TIP

2. **Use your index finger and thumb to hold the fabric in place and staple the fabric down (about 2 inches from the edge of the seat).**

    Figure 9-5 highlights this technique.

3. **Continue with this method, stapling every inch or so.**

4. **Repeat for the other sides.**

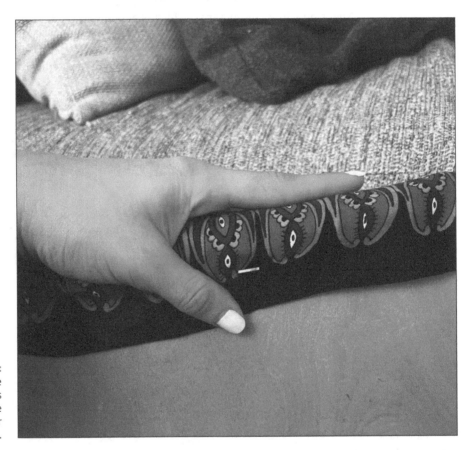

FIGURE 9-5:
Holding the fabric as shown here makes it easier to staple.

TIP

If there's a weave or pattern in your fabric, make sure to check that it's staying straight as you work.

Securing corners with pleats

Figure 9-6 highlights how to make a corner tidy with bottom pleats by using these steps:

1. **Pull tightly down the middle and staple.**

2. **Fold the fabric under the bottom, making a pleat, and then staple.**

3. **Cut away the excess fabric you don't need.**

   This makes for a tighter corner.

4. **Fold the other edge of the bottom, make another pleat, and staple.**

5. **Cut away the excess fabric.**

cut excess fabric

FIGURE 9-6:
Steps 1–4 of doing bottom corner pleats.

Trimming to trick out

Small details, such as adding upholstery trim, can really level up a piece. A decorative edge can make the contours of a chair really pop! You can buy trims or make your own cording with upcycled fabric.

For the low-fi, no-sew way to make your own cording, you need the following supplies:

>> Fabric to upcycle

>> Cotton cording (clothesline or a circular shoestring, for example)

>> Hot glue gun and glue sticks

Use Figure 9-7 as a guide for how to perform the following steps:

1. Measure the perimeter of the seat (adding the lengths of all four sides) to determine the length of cording that you need and cut enough 2" strips from your fabric to achieve that length when glued together.

2. Attach the fabric strips together by laying a strip face up and then laying another strip face down and perpendicular.

3. Add hot glue from the 90° angle down.

4. Fold and press the fabric down.

5. Trim the excess fabric.

6. Put the cording in the middle of the fabric and glue along the edge to secure it.

TIP

A hot glue gun is also perfect for attaching the cording to the bottom of the seat.

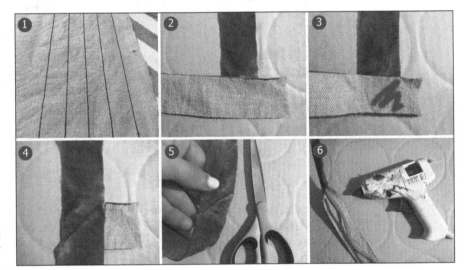

FIGURE 9-7:
Making your
own cording.

Reattaching and the big reveal

After your piece is reupholstered and trimmed, all that's left to do is reattach the base to the chair. Screw it back on or pop it in the frame (it probably will fit more tightly with new fabric) and step back to admire your masterpiece. Figure 9-8 shows the big reveal of this project.

FIGURE 9-8:
The before
and after
transformation
of this
reupholstered
dining chair.

Chapter **10**

Getting on the Cutting Edge with Glass

Glass bottles are wonderful for upcycling, which is awesome, because they're one of the easiest materials to find. Conveniently located as close as your recycling bin, wine and beer bottles are perfect for so many projects.

There's one caveat: A lot of projects require you to cut the glass bottles to repurpose them. Glass cutting may seem intimidating, but it's actually way simpler than you might think.

In this chapter, I show you how to cut glass bottles and how to drill holes in glass. These skills open up a whole new world of upcycling possibilities!

Cutting Glass Bottles with Sharp Techniques

Cutting glass bottles allows you to upcycle them in fun and creative ways. You can turn them into drinking glasses, candle holders, lights, wind chimes, planters — the list goes on because the options are endless!

Scoring leads to winning

Cutting glass involves a few steps. The first is making a single, even score line on your bottle. A *score line* is a shallow cut in the glass, and a perfect one starts and ends at the same point.

The score line creates an easy path for the glass to break along in later steps. Figure 10-1 shows an even score line.

FIGURE 10-1:
An example
of a good
score line.

TIP

To create a score line, you need either a glass cutter or a glass bottle cutting kit.

Working with a glass cutter

Glass cutters look like a pen topped with a small wheel blade. This blade is commonly made with either hardened steel or tungsten carbide. Glass cutters are inexpensive; you can find them at your local hardware store or on Amazon.

TIP

Place a strip of masking tape around your bottle and use it as a guide to create an even score line.

TIP

Another way to get an even score line is to make a jig. A *jig* is a homemade tool that helps you guide and control the glass cutter. In this instance you could rest the cutter on a flat, stable surface like the block of wood shown in Figure 10-2 and spin the bottle around to create the score line.

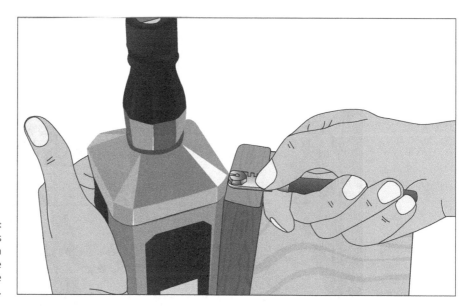

Working with a glass bottle cutting kit

If you want to cut bottles on a regular basis, it's worth investing in a glass bottle cutting kit. A kit integrates both a cutter and a jig, which makes it a lot easier to get perfect score lines. Figure 10-3 shows the Kinkajou glass bottle cutter.

TIP

If the beginning and end of your score line don't meet, move to a different place on the bottle and try again. It's important to get an even line *with one rotation only*; otherwise, the bottle won't separate nicely.

Separating the glass

Separating the glass involves really hot and cold water and the magic of science. The combination of rapidly changing temperatures causes thermal stress, cracking the bottle (ideally) along the score line.

WARNING

You should wear gloves and safety goggles when you're cutting glass to protect yourself from hot and sharp glass.

Here's how to do it:

1. **Prepare two pots of water**.

   One pot should hold boiling water and the other ice water, complete with an ice brick.

FIGURE 10-3:
Using the
Kinkajou bottle
cutter to create
an even score
line.

2. **Put the scored bottle into the boiling water.**

   Check that the bottle is getting warm by touching the glass above the water line.

3. **When the bottle feels warm to the touch, plunge it into the ice water bath.**

   The rapid cooling causes the glass to break, ideally along the score line.

4. **Repeat steps 2 and 3 as many times as necessary until the bottle separates.**

   Figure 10-4 shows how this looks.

REMEMBER

Glass isn't always predictable. Sometimes the crack occurs outside of your score line, and you have to start again.

Sanding the glass

Wet sanding is the best way to polish the cut glass edges.

WARNING

Be sure to wear goggles and a face mask for this so you don't breathe in glass particles!

FIGURE 10-4:
Bottle cut by
using hot and
cold water.

Follow these steps:

1. **Place wet, coarse sandpaper (60–80 grit), rough side up.**

2. **Rub the bottle in circular motions over the sandpaper.**

3. **Sand the inner and outer edges of the bottle.**

4. **Work your way up to higher (finer) grits of sandpaper until the bottle edges feel smooth to the touch.**

   Figure 10-5 compares a freshly cut edge with a sanded one.

Removing labels

When you first begin cutting bottles, there's a high likelihood that they won't break evenly. That's why it makes sense to wait to remove the labels until after the bottles have been cut.

Soaking the bottles in boiling water is a great way to loosen the labels, as shown in Figure 10-6. Then you can scrape them off with a butter knife.

TIP

For stubborn residue, apply Goo Gone, lighter fluid, or an even mixture of baking soda and cooking oil and let it sit for 10 minutes before rubbing it off with a scouring pad. If you use Goo Gone, remove the residue with either hot water and dish soap or isopropyl alcohol.

FIGURE 10-5:
Comparing
a freshly cut
edge (left) with
a sanded one
(right).

FIGURE 10-6:
Labels like to
come off in hot
water.

Feeling 5 o'clock fabulous

After your bottles are cut, the possibilities for what you can create are endless!
Figure 10-7 shows some ideas.

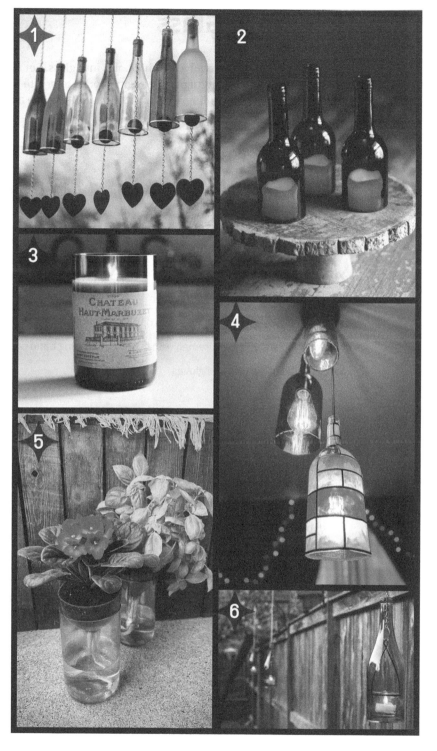

FIGURE 10-7: Cut wine bottles turned into wind chimes by Christopher Edwards of Bottles Uncorked (1), hurricane lights by Sally Behn of Wine Wicks and Gifts (2); soy wax candle by Sonny Asbury of Napa Uncorked (3), cut wine bottles turned into a pendant glass light by Judy Rom of Upcycle That (4), self-watering planters by Judy Rom of Upcycle That (5), candle lanterns by Christopher Edwards of Bottles Uncorked (6).

Drilling Holes into Glass

Lots of great DIY projects involve drilling holes into glass. For instance, you might want to add some twinkling lights to a wine bottle to create some festive decor. Figure 10-8 shows how drilling a hole by the base of a bottle allows you to thread lights through it.

The thrill of the drill

When it comes to drilling holes into glass, you need these supplies:

>> Diamond hole saw glass drill bit (see Figure 10-9)

>> Cordless drill

>> Masking tape

>> Sink to submerge object into water

>> Glass object, such as a wine bottle or a vase

>> Rotary tool (such as a Dremel) with a 120-grit sanding band or sandpaper

>> Safety gear: glasses and gloves

Here's how to do it:

1. **Add a piece of masking tape to the bottle where you want to cut it.**

   The tape helps prevent the drill from sliding around.

2. **Submerge and hold the bottle down in a tub or sink of water.**

   This prevents the glass from overheating and cracking and keeps the glass debris out of the air.

3. **Place the hole saw at a 45° angle and begin drilling.**

   This gives the drill bit a chance to catch the glass.

4. **Move the drill bit into a more upright position and move it around in a circular motion.**

   Use light pressure only, and let the weight of the drill do the work. After the bit breaks through the glass, the hole is complete.

5. **Use either a Dremel with a sanding band, or sandpaper to smooth down the sharp edges.**

FIGURE 10-8:
Create simple and effective decor. Tim and Mary Vidra of 17 Apart made these lights.

FIGURE 10-9:
A diamond
hole saw is
designed to
drill holes into
glass.

Drilling drainage holes

Adding a hole for drainage allows you to turn practically any container into a plant pot.

To do this, you need the following items:

>> Ceramic or masonry drill bit (see Figure 10-10)

>> Drill

>> Safety gear: goggles, dust mask, ear protection

>> Ceramic pot or glass container

Here's how to do it:

1. **Put on your safety gear and flip the container upside down.**

2. **Keep a solid grip on the pot, insert the drill bit, and begin drilling with moderate pressure.**

3. **Ease up on the pressure when the drill bit catches, and drill with a consistent and medium speed until the hole is complete.**

FIGURE 10-10:
A ceramic
or masonry
bit has an
arrow-shaped
tip that's wider
than its shaft.

Chapter **11**

Reclaimed to Fame Wood

Reclaimed wood is the darling of the upcycling world. Upcyclers are down-right obsessed with it, and for good reason. Simply put, reclaimed wood is gorgeous.

Reclaimed wood has already had a previous life. It may have been a pallet, boat, barn, or building. This wood is rich with character, and instantly adds rustic charm to your projects. It's also environmentally savvy because it saves these materials from ending up in a landfill.

In this chapter, I share where to source reclaimed wood. The great news is that once you start looking for reclaimed wood, you'll begin to notice it everywhere. For example, pallets are free and widely available. Consequently, this chapter also covers what to look for in a pallet and the best techniques for taking them apart. Last but not least, I offer some inspiration for what you can make with pallets.

Bringing Old Wood Back to Life

Reclaimed wood has the interesting visual character that comes from being weathered over time. This wood has already lived a life. It may have come from the beams of an old barn or been recovered from a broken fence on the side of a road.

Timber is expensive, and reclaimed wood is an awesome way to get usable lumber for less. What may look dilapidated could actually be a goldmine of old growth. Figure 11-1 highlights the stunning charm of reclaimed wood.

FIGURE 11-1: The weathered beauty of reclaimed wood.

Sourcing reclaimed wood

You can source paid or free reclaimed wood in multiple places. Here are some options:

» Construction sites, dumpsters, and contractors

» Demolition sites

» Farms that are demolishing old buildings

» Grocery stores and distribution centers that discard pallets

» Reclaimed lumberyards

>> Architectural salvage dealers

>> Recycling and reuse centers

>> Online marketplaces like Craigslist and Facebook Marketplace

TIP

Try searching online for *salvaged wood*, *reclaimed wood*, *reclaimed lumber*, *reclaimed timber*, or *barnwood* to find a source near you.

WARNING

Always ask for permission before taking wood from someone's property. They might be thrilled that someone wants it, but you won't know for sure unless you ask!

Giving new life to old boards

When working with reclaimed wood, it's important to have a clear idea of what you want to create before starting. Working with reclaimed wood is a bit more complicated than working with virgin wood. That's because the wood will likely be of varying lengths and may have previous cuts or defects in it. Don't let that deter you. It simply means you need to do some planning.

Here are the preparatory steps:

1. **Decide what project you'll be creating.**

2. **Determine how much wood you need and plan for having 20 percent.**

3. **Find a source for the reclaimed wood.**

4. **Clean and de-nail the wood.**

TIP

   More expensive reclaimed wood will likely be clean and nail-free. However, if you have the time to clean and remove nails, you can find free wood and put in the elbow grease.

TIP

   Nails can really mess up power tools. It's a great idea to buy a woodworking metal detector to check for hidden metal in the wood. Detectors are inexpensive and can save you from inflecting some seriously costly damage. You can find them at hardware stores.

5. **Make your cuts.**

   Cut your prepared reclaimed wood to the required lengths for your project.

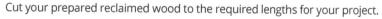

TIP

   The best part of using reclaimed wood is the character it already has. Plan your cuts in a way to showcase the cool and distinctive parts.

6. **Label your cuts with a pencil as you go.**

   This helps you remember what goes where.

7. **Sand your wood.**

   Work with progressively higher/finer grits, going up to 320–400 so that it's nice and smooth to the touch.

Giving Pallets a Second Life

Pallets are the most readily available source of reclaimed wood. If it seems like they can be found just about everywhere, it's because they can. Pallets are essential to transporting goods. It's a bit mind-boggling to think, but almost every product comes delivered on a pallet. Using forklifts to load cargo is what makes trucking and shipping possible, and without pallets, forklifting wouldn't be feasible. Pallets are the backbone of the transportation industry.

Luckily for upcyclers, pallets are abundant and free. You can transform them into furniture, art, walls, you name it. They're really the sweethearts of the upcycling world. But before you run out and pick up the very next pallet you see, know that not all pallets are created equal. Figure 11-2 shows some pallets waiting to be discovered.

FIGURE 11-2:
Pallets ready
for the taking.

Picking a pallet

When it comes to picking a pallet, keep these factors in mind for finding and using the best ones:

>> **Condition:** Due to the nature of what pallets are used for, they can sustain damage during shipping or be the victims of spills. The first thing to look at when selecting a pallet is its condition. Look for a pallet that's solid, with no breakage or nasty stains on it.

>> **Size:** Pallets come in multiple sizes. In North America, the standard pallet size is 48" × 40".

TIP

When sourcing pallet(s) for your project, think about what you're making and then choose pallets that fit the bill size-wise.

>> **Styles:** The two main categories of pallets are stringers and blocks. Stringers have a two-way entry and blocks have a four-way entry. Figure 11-3 illustrates this distinction.

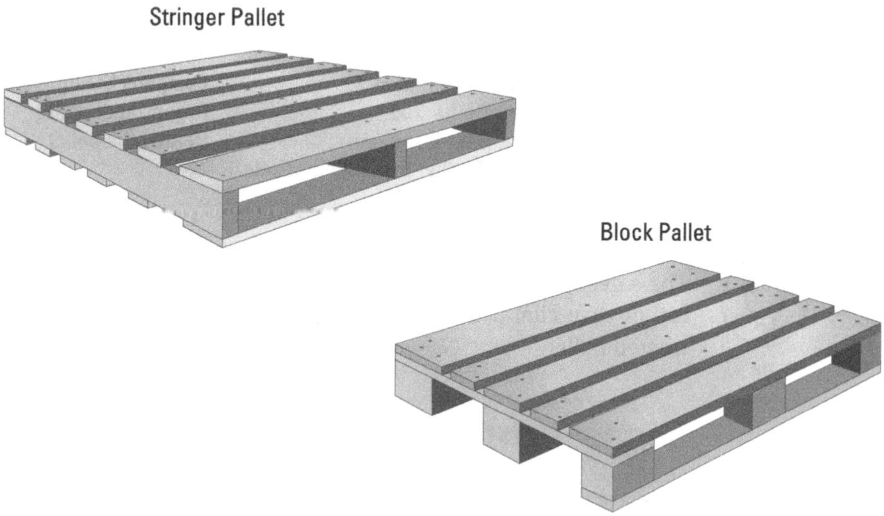

Stringer Pallet

Block Pallet

FIGURE 11-3:
Stringers and blocks, the two main types of pallets.

Not all pallets are safe for upcycling. Because they're used to transport food, pallets are treated to prevent bugs and disease. It's important to look at the markings on the pallet to see what kind of treatment has been done.

Figure 11-4 explains what the different codes on pallet markings mean.

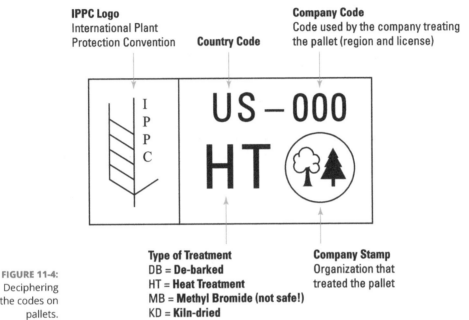

IPPC Logo
International Plant
Protection Convention

Country Code

Company Code
Code used by the company treating
the pallet (region and license)

Type of Treatment
DB = **De-barked**
HT = **Heat Treatment**
MB = **Methyl Bromide (not safe!)**
KD = **Kiln-dried**

Company Stamp
Organization that
treated the pallet

FIGURE 11-4:
Deciphering
the codes on
pallets.

TIP

The safest pallet to use is HT, which means the pallet has been treated with heat rather than chemicals. Figure 11-5 shows an example of the marking on a heat-treated pallet.

Disassembling a pallet

Here are the two ways that consistently work:

The circular saw method

This is a reliably quick way to disassemble a pallet. You lose a bit of length on the ends, but you save a lot of time in nail removal because you literally cut most of the nailed parts out!

With this technique you need just a few things:

>> Circular saw

>> Crow/pry bar

>> Hammer

>> Nail punch (optional)

Here's how to do it:

1. **Set the depth of your circular saw to the thickness of the slats.**

2. **Run the saw straight along the inside edge of the nails.**

   Do this to the outer edges of the pallet. Figure 11-6 shows this step.

3. **Flip the pallet over and do the same to the backside.**

4. **Remove the pallet deck planks from the center stringer with your hammer and pry bar.**

   Figure 11-7 illustrates the technique.

5. **Repeat step 4 until you've removed all the boards from the stringer.**

6. **Use your hammer or a nail punch to remove the nails from the center of the planks. A nail punch is a handy tool that makes removing bent nails a breeze.**

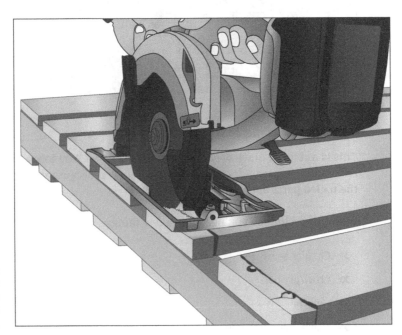

FIGURE 11-6:
This is where to cut with your circular saw.

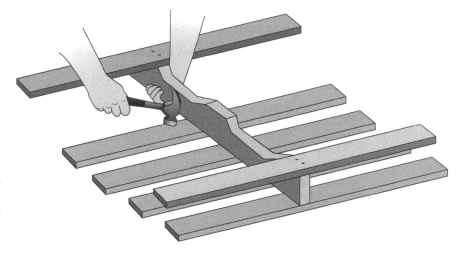

The hammer and four blocks of wood method

This is a great low-fi technique if you want to keep the full length of the board or you don't have a circular saw.

With this technique you need just two things:

>> Four blocks of wood (pieces of 2" × 4" work well)

>> Sledgehammer or hammer

Here's how to do it:

1. **Lay two blocks lengthwise on either side of the pallet deck plank that you're trying to remove.**

2. **Place the third block on top of the first two blocks, *underneath* the pallet deck plank.**

3. **Place the fourth block on the stringer (the outer piece of the pallet) and hit the block with your sledgehammer or hammer.**

   This loosens the nails of the pallet deck from the stringer. Figure 11-8 shows how this looks.

4. Repeat steps 1 through 3 until the whole pallet is disassembled.

5. Turn the boards upside down and hammer the bottom of the nails to remove them.

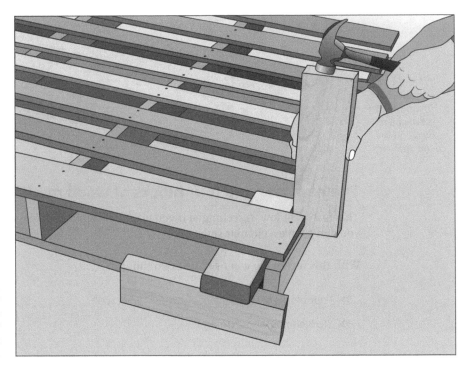

Divining Pallet Inspiration

The application for pallets is endless. You can use them to create tables, chairs, shelves, bed frames, crates, planters, signs, walls, and more. The list goes on and on.

Figure 11-9 shows just a few examples of the types of pieces you can create from pallets.

FIGURE 11-9:
Pallets can
be used for
upcycling in
numerous
ways!

4

Upcycling Tutorials for Your Home

Follow furniture tutorials to create specific upcycled furniture looks, including a desk, coffee table, bar, chair, and two different side tables.

Add character and class with easy-to-follow upcycling tutorials for home decor and upcycled art.

Shine the spotlight on upcycled lighting and create two new pieces.

Bring more greenery to your life. Learn how to make fun planters using wine corks and bottles.

Chapter **12**

Reimagining Furniture

U pcycling saves furniture from the landfill and results in pieces that are completely unique.

In this chapter, I show you how to make six upcycled furniture projects. I break these projects down step by step so that you can easily replicate them.

Chevron-Inspired Desk

This chevron-inspired desk is an homage to the stylish zig-zag pattern popularly used for home decor. You may have seen chevron textiles, backsplashes, and hardwood floors. This upcycled desk is a nod to that.

The chevron-inspired motif is a superb way to dress up a plain ole desk. The flat white paint looks fresh and sleek, and the woodgrain shines through in the negative spaces (that aren't painted over). The top of Figure 12-1 shows the original desk. The bottom of Figure 12-1 shows the result.

FIGURE 12-1:
This chevron-inspired design looks fabulous as a desk!

Here's what you need to make it:

TIP

TIP

>> **A desk to upcycle**

This design will work on many desks or as a coffee table. Try searching on Facebook Marketplace to find a good one.

>> **300-grit sandpaper**

>> **Tack cloth**

>> **Painter's tape**

I recommend FrogTape brand painter's tape because it prevents paint bleed.

>> **Measuring tape or yardstick**

>> **Hobby knife**

>> **Ruler**

>> **Paintable (not silicone-based) caulk**

>> **White chalk paint**

>> **Paint roller**

>> **Angled brush**

>> **Sealant**

>> **Gold accent paint** (optional)

Here's how to apply the chevron design:

1. **Clean and prepare the desk.**

   Give the desk a solid clean. Wipe it down with a sudsy rag and vacuum out the drawers. Then lightly sand the wood and wipe away the sanding residue with a tack cloth.

2. **Determine where to put the Vs.**

   Measure the width of the desk and divide it by two to determine where the middle point of the Vs will go. Add your first row of tape. Figure 12-2 illustrates this.

3. **Add the rest of the taped design.**

   Placing tape temporarily between rows is a wonderful way to get perfectly spaced lines without having to measure. Figure 12-3 highlights this technique.

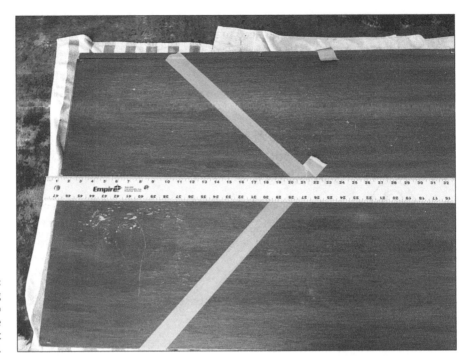

FIGURE 12-2:
Measuring
the desk to
determine the
middle point
for the Vs.

FIGURE 12-3:
Using the
tape to
measure
out lines.

4. Trim the tape.

Work with a ruler and a hobby knife to trim the edges of the tape (see Figure 12-4).

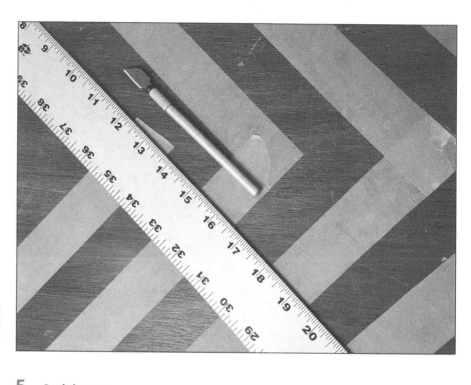

FIGURE 12-4:
Use a ruler and knife to tidy up the lines.

5. Seal the tape.

Put a narrow bead of caulk around the edges of the tape and use a small brush to spread it as shown in Figure 12-5. The caulk fills in any spaces where the paint could bleed through and makes the lines crisp.

REMEMBER

Make sure the caulk *is not* made of silicone and says that it is paintable.

6. Paint the desk.

Apply two coats of chalk paint on the desk surface, including on top of the tape. Allow the paint to dry fully between coats. Figure 12-6 shows the desk in-progress.

7. Peel off the painter's tape.

Wait until the paint has fully dried and then slowly and steadily pull the painter's tape back on itself (at a 45° angle). If the paint starts to lift with the tape, use a sharp knife to score along the edge of the tape.

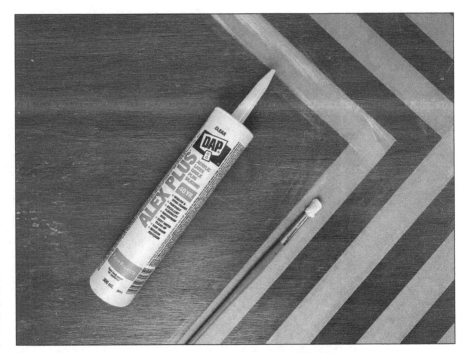

FIGURE 12-5:
Using caulk
like this makes
the paint lines
crisp and
smooth.

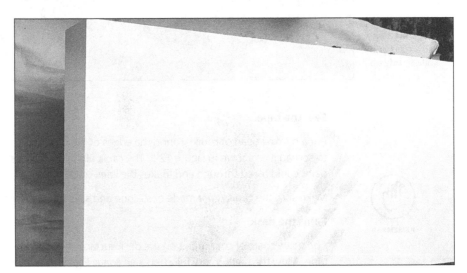

FIGURE 12-6:
Chalk paint is
smooth and
easy to use.

8. **Add accents.**

   This piece was badly scratched, and wood veneer can only be lightly sanded. So, I added gold accents with dabs of gold paint to cover it up, as shown in the left side of Figure 12-7.

The key to adding accents is to underload the brush with paint and lightly dab it onto the wood.

9. Finish the table.

Seal the desk with two to three coats of sealant. Allow the paint to fully dry between coats. Read Chapter 6 for information about sealing.

It's worth the effort to triple-seal high-traffic pieces to ensure they last. Use thin, light coats.

10. Reassemble the desk.

Admire your new chevron-inspired desk! The right side of Figure 12-7 shows the finished result.

FIGURE 12-7: The gold paint details add dimension and cover up the scratches (left). The finished chevron-style desk is a real beauty (right)!

Drawer-Turned Desk

Sometimes you happen upon a broken piece of furniture and only a piece of it is salvageable. Or, as with this project, you might find a lone dresser drawer in an alley (see the top of Figure 12-8).

FIGURE 12-8:
This drawer
was found in
a back alley
(top). This
drawer-turned
coffee table
is perfect for
displaying
a collection
(bottom).

To make this coffee table, you need the following supplies:

>> A drawer to upcycle

>> A piece of glass cut to size

>> Silicone caulk

>> Hairpin legs

>> Velvet to inlay in the drawer

>> Cardboard to back the velvet

>> A collection to display in the drawer (optional)

TIP

Your local glass and window shop can cut a piece of glass to the appropriate size.

Here's how to make your coffee table:

1. **Prepare the drawer.**

   Give it a solid clean. Wipe it down and leave it as is or sand, stain, and seal it.

2. **Inlay the drawer with velvet.**

   Measure the inside of the drawer and cut a piece of cardboard to size. Then cover the cardboard with velvet, place tape on the back of the cardboard, and put the velvet-covered cardboard in the drawer.

3. **Attach the glass to the drawer with silicone caulk.**

   Add a bead of caulk around the top edges of the drawer and place the glass on top. Add some heavy books to weigh it down as the caulk sets.

4. **Add hairpin legs.**

   Drill the hairpin legs onto the base of the drawer. These can be sourced online from Amazon.com or salvaged from another piece of furniture.

5. **Display a collection (optional).**

   This style of coffee table is perfect for exhibiting an assemblage of your favorite things. The bottom of Figure 12-8 shows the completed coffee table housing a batch of vintage stir sticks.

Steamer Trunk Bar

Classy, sophisticated, and stunning, this steamer trunk bar is the crème de-la-crème with sprinkles and a cherry on top. It's sure to be the focal point of any room it graces. See all of its glory in Figure 12-9.

FIGURE 12-9:
The majestic
and gorgeous
steamer
trunk bar.

You'll need the following materials and tools to make one:

- Old trunk
- Hairpin legs
- Sheet of ½" plywood
- Sheet of ¼" plywood
- Sheet of ⅛" plywood
- Glass cut to size and bordered with mirror trim

  Have your local window and glass shop cut the glass and add the mirror trim.
- Wood glue
- Epoxy adhesive
- Wood filler
- Wipe-on poly sealant
- Nails
- Sandpaper in 150, 220, and 320 grits
- Square
- Chop saw
- Table saw
- Jigsaw
- Nail gun
- Clamps
- Rag
- Level
- Router drill bit and drill (optional)

1. **Measure the dimensions of the inner trunk and cut the ¼" plywood to line the bottom and sides and the ½" plywood for the shelves of the trunk.**

2. **Sand the plywood.**

   First use the 150-grit, then the 220-grit, and then the 320-grit sandpaper.

3. **Square the sides of the box and assemble it with wood glue and a nail gun.**

   Asking a friend to assist you with this step makes it much easier.

TIP

   You can use a carpenter's square to check that you've made your corners perfectly square. Stick the tool into each corner to determine whether it truly is a 90-degree angle.

4. **Level and square the shelves.**

   Attach them with wood glue and a nail gun. Figure 12-10 shows how the shelves and inner wooden frame look at this point.

TIP

   The height of your shelves is up to you. The ones pictured here have a 14" height for the bottom shelf and an 8" height for the second shelf.

If you want to have room for taller bottles, you can do a cutout in your shelf. To do this optional step, measure where you want the cut and use a router drill bit to make a hole in the corner. Then cut into the hole from either side using a table saw. Sand the edges of the plywood to smooth.

FIGURE 12-10:
The plywood frame and shelves will line the inside of the steamer trunk bar.

5. **Fill in the gaps in the edges of the plywood.**

   Use wood filler for this. Allow it to dry completely, and then sand it.

6. **Jigsaw out the top of the trunk.**

   Measure in 1½" from the metal border and use a jigsaw to cut out the top of the trunk, as shown in Figure 12-11.

7. **Glue the mirror-trim-bordered glass into the space that you created.**

   Use an epoxy adhesive for this. Tape it down to keep it secure while it sets, as shown in Figure 12-12.

FIGURE 12-11:
Cutting out
the top of the
steamer trunk
with a jigsaw.

FIGURE 12-12:
Securing the
glass to the top
of the steamer
trunk.

8. Attach the plywood base and frame.

Glue the ¼" plywood base as well as the inner plywood frame into the trunk with wood glue. Use clamps to secure it, as shown in Figure 12-13. Allow it to dry overnight.

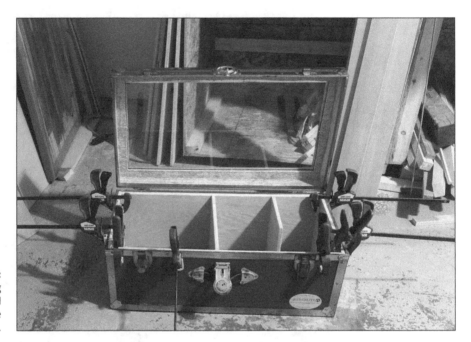

9. Trim the inside top of the trunk with ⅛" plywood.

Measure and cut the plywood trim so that it borders the glass on the inside of the trunk lid. Attach it with wood glue and clamps and allow it to dry before staining. Figure 12-14 shows the inside of the trunk with the plywood trim in place.

TIP

Cut plywood at 45-degree angles to frame the inside of the trunk's window.

FIGURE 12-14:
The ⅛"
plywood lines
the inside of
the glass to
finish the look.

10. **Add hairpin legs to the bottom of the steamer trunk.**

Once the legs are on, the bar is ready to stock and serve. Figure 12-15 shows the finished look.

Industrial Side Table

Sometimes a found item just needs a little TLC and some hairpin legs to become a side table. Like this discovered card file cabinet in Figure 12-16.

To make this industrial side table you will need:

>> A card file cabinet to upcycle

>> 300-grit sandpaper

>> Tack cloth

- Painter's tape
- Paint
- Paintbrushes and roller
- Sealant
- Drill and drill bits
- Hairpin legs

TIP

Online classifieds, vintage stores, Etsy, and eBay are all good places to look for card file cabinets to upcycle.

Here's how to make your industrial side table:

1. **Prepare the cabinet.**

    Clean it out and remove the hardware (if possible) or cover the hardware with painter's tape. Then lightly sand the surface to help the paint adhere. The top of Figure 12-17 shows this stage.

2. **Apply the primer.**

    Apply two to three coats of primer. This really helps the paint stick and makes it appear more vibrant. The bottom left of Figure 12-17 shows the primed cabinet.

FIGURE 12-17:
The cabinet
is sanded
and taped
and ready for
primer (top).
Primed and
ready for paint
(bottom left).
The painting
process
(bottom right).

3. **Paint.**

   Apply two to three thin coats of paint. Allow the paint to dry fully between coats, and lightly sand to remove any paint drips. Then remove the sanding dust with a tack cloth. The bottom right of Figure 12-17 shows the cabinet mid-painting.

4. **Finish.**

   Remove the tape from the handles and seal the piece.

TIP

Use a blade to scrape off any paint that might've gotten onto the handle.

5. Predrill the holes for the screws.

Mark where the holes will go, and then predrill the holes as shown in Figure 12-18.

Predrilling the holes is essential for screwing into metal.

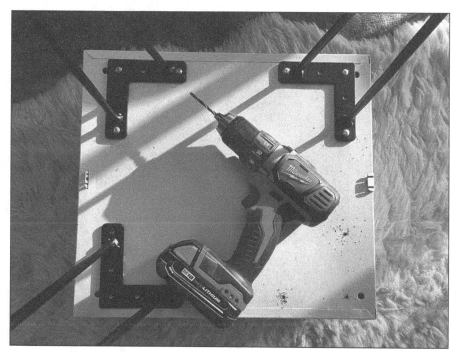

FIGURE 12-18:
Predrilling the holes to attach the legs.

6. Screw on the hairpin legs.

After you've attached the legs, your industrial side table is good to go! Figure 12-19 shows the completed piece.

FIGURE 12-19:
The card file cabinet is now an industrial side table.

Victorian-Style Parlor Chair

There's something timeless about well-appointed, high-back parlor chairs. The one in Figure 12-20 has magnificent details with a crest of roses and cabriole legs. Look up "good bones," and you'll find a picture of this chair. With all these gorgeous details, it was ripe for revitalization.

FIGURE 12-20: The armchair prior to upcycling (left). Lining painter's tape around the edge of the frame to safeguard the upholstery from paint drips (right).

TIP

Scoop up well-priced vintage pieces at garage and estate sales.

To rejuvenate an armchair like this you will need:

- An armchair
- Painter's tape
- 220- and 400-grit sandpaper
- Tack cloth
- Primer
- Paint
- Paintbrushes

- » Gold leaf and size/glue

- » Sealant

- » Crystal buttons

- » E6000 glue

Here's how to revitalize the chair:

1. **Sand.**

   Give the chair a light sand with 220-grit sandpaper to prepare it for priming. Clean up the sanding dust with a tack cloth.

2. **Tape.**

   Use painter's tape to protect the upholstery from paint. The right side of Figure 12-20 shows the taped chair.

3. **Apply the primer.** When painting over dark wood with a light color, two to three coats of primer is ideal. The primer allows good coverage and prevents bleed-through.

4. **Paint.**

   Apply two coats of paint. For this chair, I used the Rust-oleum metallic accent in Pearl. Lightly sand between coats with 400-grit sandpaper.

5. **Gild.**

   Gold leaf is perfect for bringing out the luxurious nature of this ornate chair. See Chapter 5 for the details of how to use gold leaf with size/glue. Figure 12-21 shows a close-up of the gold foil accents.

6. **Seal.** Finish the gold leaf with sealant.

7. **Remove the painter's tape.**

   Touch up the paint as necessary with a painter's brush.

   A sharp blade is great for removing any pooled paint edges.

8. **Add embellishments.**

   The final touch is adding crystal buttons. The original buttons were deeply recessed, so I used E6000 adhesive to glue the new ones right on top. The left side of Figure 12-22 reveals the finished look. The right side of Figure 12-22 shows a close-up of the gold leaf details.

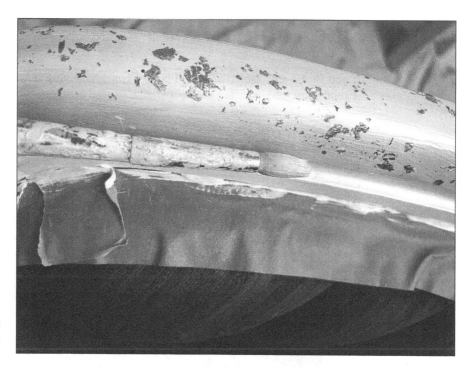

FIGURE 12-21: Gilding with gold leaf.

FIGURE 12-22: The Victorian armchair reigns again (left). The gold leaf highlights the ornate hand carvings (right).

Ombre Side Table

If you find a side table with good bones, consider giving it an ombre paint job. A good paint job can really go the distance!

Figure 12-23 shows the side table before upcycling.

FIGURE 12-23: This scratched-up side table was ready for an upgrade (left). The finished look of the gorgeous ombre side table (right).

To create an ombre look on a side table, you will need:

>> A side table

>> 220- and 400-grit sandpaper

>> Tack cloth

>> Primer

>> Paint

>> Paintbrushes

>> Sealant

Here's how to paint the table:

1. **Sand.**

   Use 220-grit sandpaper to prepare the table for priming. Remove the sanding dust with a tack cloth.

2. **Prime.**

   Apply two coats of primer.

3. **Paint.**

   Paint the top and bottom of the table in their respective colors. Allow the paint to dry, and then paint a second coat for each. The left of Figure 12-24 shows this step.

FIGURE 12-24: Color-blocking the paint prior to blending (left). Using a paint roller makes blending super easy (top right). Rolling the colors together to create the ombre (bottom right).

4. **Prepare to blend.**

   Load a roller with both colors in the order used on the piece. The top right of Figure 12-24 shows a roller prepped with white and blue paints.

5. **Blend.**

   Pass the roller back and forth over the piece where the two colors meet until you achieve your desired look. The bottom right of Figure 12-24 shows the blending. Chapter 5 offers more detail on this technique.

6. **Seal.**

   Complete the revamp with sealant. See the finished look on the right side of Figure 12-23.

Chapter **13**

Elevating a Room with Home Decor

I f you're looking to elevate your interior style, home decor is a phenomenal way to do it. This category includes items like cushions, trays, plants, mirrors, and art that makes your home visually appealing. Think of it as the accessories to your furnishings. These finishing touches contribute to the overall *aesthetic* of your space and really tie a room together.

Home decor encompasses the details that make your house a home. In this chapter, I share what you should consider when selecting home decor. I also explain how to make three home decor items: teacup candles, tiered trays, and mountain-shaped shelves. The items are functional and add ambience.

How to Choose Home Decor

In a nutshell, home decor is what makes your home lovely and inviting. What you choose is an extension of your personal style and who you are. There are no strict rules, but here are some ideas to guide you:

>> **Think about how you want the room to feel.** Choose a few words to describe the vibe you want to create. For instance, if you want a *cozy space*, it makes sense to include lots of soft textures like throw blankets and cushions.

>> **Choose a theme.** Perhaps you love the sea. In this case, you might want to have a beach theme with elements like ocean photography and seashell-shaped cushions.

>> **Embrace a style or an era.** If you love a certain design style, you can align your home decor to match. Or, if you like to travel, you could embrace a bohemian theme and incorporate textiles and souvenirs from your travels.

>> **Pick a palette.** Basing your decor around your favorite colors is a great way to keep your look cohesive.

>> **Highlight a central piece.** If you have a statement piece in mind, like a large painting or rug, you can coordinate the rest of the room's elements to match.

TIP

Fill your home with joy by choosing items that make you happy.

Teacup Candles

Candles are one of the best ways to add ambience. Teacup candles are extra lovely because they use gorgeous, repurposed teacups. You can light up an elegant tea party at the strike of a match! Figure 13-1 showcases their beauty.

Here's what you need to make them:

>> Vintage teacups

>> Soy wax pellets

Alternatively, you can chop up and reuse wax remnants provided they are all the same kind of wax — that is, all soy or all beeswax.

>> Soy wax-coated candle wicks in a size that's taller than the container you're pouring into

>> Essential oils

FIGURE 13-1:
Teacup
candles add
an enchanting
energy.

>> Hot glue gun with glue

>> Double boiler or two pots

>> Tape or candle wick holders

>> Scissors

TIP

You might already have some teacups ready for upcycling. Otherwise, you can source them at thrift stores and garage sales. Be sure to wash and dry them thoroughly before repurposing.

When you have your supplies gathered, you're ready to get to work on the following steps:

1. **Melt the wax.**

   Use a double-boiler, or stack one pot with the wax on top of another that holds hot water. Turn the heat to medium and allow the wax to melt as you occasionally give it a stir. The top left of Figure 13-2 shows how to do this.

FIGURE 13-2:
Melting the wax with the double-boiler technique (top left). Gluing the wicks in place keeps them secure when you pour the hot wax in (top right). Bordering with tape keeps the wicks in place once the wax is poured (bottom left). The teacup candles after they've been poured (bottom right).

TIP

Using the double-boiler technique ensures that the wax fully melts instead of burning.

2. **Glue the wicks in place**.

Using a hot glue gun, add a dot of glue beneath the wick and place it in the center of the bottom of the teacup. The top right of Figure 13-2 shows the wicks glued into place.

3. **Add tape supports outside the wick.**

The wicks will want to slip and slide around. Using tape (or wick holders) as shown in the bottom left of Figure 13-2 keeps them anchored.

4. **Let the wax cool for two to three minutes and then add in the essential oils.**

The wax needs to cool a bit; otherwise, the heat mutes the scent of the essential oils. Stir in the essential oils of your choice. You need to add 2 teaspoons of oil for every 4 ounces of melted wax.

5. **Pour the melted wax into your containers.**

Carefully pour the melted wax into the teacups. If your wicks start tipping, you can add more tape, as shown in the bottom right of Figure 13-2.

6. **Allow the wax to fully harden.**

Putting the candles in the fridge can speed up this step. Once the wax has set, you can remove the tape and trim the wicks to about ½ inch above the wax. Figure 13-3 shows the wicks post-trimming.

FIGURE 13-3: Trimming the wicks after the wax has set.

7. Light the candles.

The teacup candles are now ready for use. Figure 13-4 shows the beautiful ambiance of one burning.

FIGURE 13-4:
Teacup candle
in action.

Tiered Trays

Tiered trays are a fun upcycle made with repurposed plates and glasses. They look glamorous and can be used in a few different ways. Tiered trays are the perfect way to serve treats at a party, and they're fabulous for organizing and displaying jewelry. Figure 13-5 shows a tantalizing three-tiered tray heaped with goodies.

FIGURE 13-5:
A gorgeous, three-tiered tray is superb for hosting.

Making a tiered tray is a nice and simple upcycle. You need the following materials:

>> Two or three plates

>> One or two glasses or cups

>> E6000 glue

Find plates and glassware that you love and want to show off. Cut crystal is particularly stunning for tiered trays. You may already have some pieces; otherwise, look for them at garage sales and thrift stores.

Play around with the dishes to see how they look stacked together. You can even do this at the thrift shop before you buy them, as shown in the top left of Figure 13-6.

Follow these steps to make a tiered tray:

1. **Wash and dry the dishes thoroughly.**

2. **Apply the E6000 glue to the surfaces that you're bonding.**

   Make sure to put glue only where the connecting pieces touch and center the pieces. You can place a book on top to add some weight while the adhesive is drying, but be careful not to nudge it off-center. The top right of Figure 13-6 shows the E6000 being used on the glassware.

3. **Allow 24–72 hours for the glue to cure.**

   E6000 takes a while to set, so you need to put your glued pieces in a safe place where they can cure undisturbed for at least a day. The bottom of Figure 13-6 shows the set tiered tray, ready for use.

4. **Style for use.**

   These tiered trays are brilliant for serving platters. They're so dramatically gorgeous! Figure 13-7 shows off the finished piece, including a couple other variations that were made to be jewelry organizers.

FIGURE 13-6:
Trying different
combinations
of plates and
glasses (top
left). E6000
glue in use
(top right).
The tiered tray
is now glued
and cured
(bottom).

FIGURE 13-7:
The tiered tray
in use (top).
It also makes
for a fantastic
jewelry
organizer
(bottom).

Mountain Shelves

Mountain shelves are a lovely accent piece for the wall. You can use them to home crystals, jewelry, or any other "smalls," as shown in Figure 13-8.

FIGURE 13-8: Mountain shelves are an ideal way to display a collection of crystals or other small objects.

TIP

Make your mountain shelves with reclaimed wood.

You need the following supplies:

>> Reclaimed wood. This reclaimed wood came from an unwanted bookshelf that had been discarded in an alley. The wood from it was 26" × 10" and ¾" thick, but you can work with any dimensions to make this.

>> Table saw. You might not need a saw if your wood already has your desired depth.

>> Miter saw.

>> Brad nailer or nails and a hammer.

>> Carpenter square.

>> Measuring tape.

>> Wood glue.

>> Sandpaper.

>> Propane torch (optional).

>> Pencil.

>> Tung oil or sealant of your choice.

1. **Choose a depth for your wood.**

   How much do you want your shelves to stand out from the wall? The wood I used was cut to 5" deep using a table saw. Figure 13-9 shows the boards after I'd cut them.

FIGURE 13-9: Cut boards for the mountain shelves.

2. **Decide on the dimensions you want your mountains to be and cut the wood accordingly.**

   Figure 13-10 shows the dimensions I used.

TIP

   If your wood isn't long enough, you can join two boards. Do this by drilling holes and adding dowels and securing with wood glue. See Figure 13-11 for a reference image.

FIGURE 13-10:
The dimensions of the wood used for this set of mountain shelves.

3. **Cut the ends of the wood to 45-degree angles using a miter saw.**

TIP

   Use a carpenter square to measure the angle and mark it with a pencil, as shown in Figure 13-12.

4. **Put the mountain shelves together using a brad nailer and wood glue.**

TIP

   Ideally you want to have a friend assisting with this step. One person can hold the wood in place, while the other one nails.

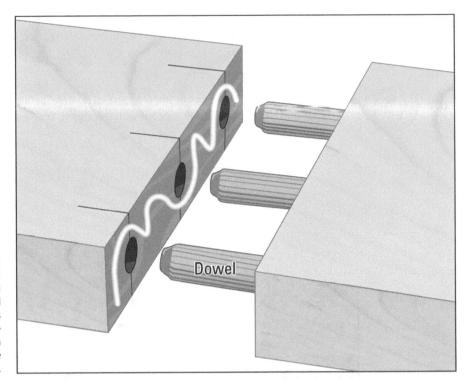

FIGURE 13-11:
Drill holes in the ends of the boards and add dowels and wood glue so you can connect the pieces.

Dowel

FIGURE 13-12:
The sides marked and cut to 45-degree angles.

5. **Cut the inner shelves to fit and cut the ends to 45-degree angles.**

The lengths you need for the inner shelves are specific to the dimensions of the wood you're using. The dimensions of the mountain shelves shown in Figure 13-13 follow:

- **Shelves for the smaller peaks:** 6 ¼" length cut to a 45-degree point on one side and 45-degree angle on the other

- **Top shelf in the middle peak:** 5 ½" length with 45-degree angles

- **Middle shelf in the middle peak:** 10 ¼" length with 45-degree angles

- **Bottom shelf in the middle peak:** 6 ¾" length with 45-degree angles

- **Angled shelves in the middle peak:** 6 ¾" length with a 45-degree angle on one side and a 90-degree angle on the other

FIGURE 13-13: The inner shelves are cut to fit inside the mountain peaks.

6. **Attach the inner shelves with a brad nailer and wood glue.**

Allow the glue to dry completely.

7. **(Optional step) Patina the shelves with stain or use a propane torch.**

Propane torches are a fun tool that can bring out the natural beauty of the wood grain. It's similar to a lighter but has a slightly bigger flame. To use a propane torch, ignite it and hold it 2" to 3" above the wood. Pass it over the wood in the direction of the wood grain. The longer you apply it, the darker the wood will become.

8. **Lightly sand the shelves and seal them with a finish of your choice.**

9. **Hang the mountain shelves and style them as you wish.**

TIP

Have a friend hold the mountain shelves on the wall and use a pencil to mark the inside corners. Add nails on the marked spots to securely hang the shelves.

Chapter **14**

Shining the Spotlight on Lamps

L ight up your life with upcycled lighting! Upcycled lights add a warm and wonderful ambience. They are like glowing pieces of functional art. The best part? There are so many ways to create them.

In this chapter, I offer two options for upcycled lighting. The first shows you how to make a fire truck lamp from an upcycled toy. This industrial light is so joyful, especially exciting for little people who love trucks.

The second lighting tutorial is a pendant lamp made with cut wine bottles. Curb-side recycling is dramatically transformed! This upcycle also features a lustrous stained-glass effect, which is a brilliant method to turn any clear glass bottle into a gleaming work of art. In addition, I include directions for wiring and suspending a lamp. With these newfound skills, both you and your light will be shining bright!

Fire Truck Lamp

The fire truck lamp is perfect for kids (big and small), that are obsessed with trucks. It's also one of the easiest upcycles in the book! Making it an ideal project for people who like maximum impact with minimal effort.

Here's what you need for this super cool project:

>> A toy fire truck

>> A pendant light

   A pendant is a single light fixture that suspends from the ceiling. You can
   purchase them at hardware stores or on Amazon.

>> An Edison bulb (I used 60W)

>> A pendant cage (optional)

>> Double-sided adhesive/snot tape

TIP

You may already have a fire truck you can use. Otherwise, keep an eye out at thrift
stores and garage sales.

Figure 14-1 shows a fire truck ready to answer the upcycling call.

FIGURE 14-1:
Something like
this is a perfect
candidate for
being turned
into a lamp.

Once you have your materials, here's how to get upcycling:

1. **Give the fire truck a solid cleaning with warm water and dish soap.**

2. **Run the pendant light cord over the top of the fire truck ladder**.

   If you see places to integrate the cord with the truck, do that. For instance, you
   can run the cord through a loop or weave it around a ladder rung. Figure 14-2
   shows how I ran the cord through a loop.

3. **Install the bulb and cage (if you're using one).**

   A cage really finishes the look of the lamp and completes the industrial
   aesthetic on the left of Figure 14-3. It's also a nice safety feature to keep little
   fingers from touching hot bulbs.

4. **Streamline the look of the cord by affixing it onto the truck.**

   Try using double-sided adhesive (often called snot tape or boogie glue) that's
   sticky, rubbery, and meant for holding items in place. It'll hold on, but it won't
   muck up the cord permanently. The right side of Figure 14-3 shows the cord
   "snotted" in place. A dab of glue also works in a pinch.

FIGURE 14-3:
The installed
light bulb and
cage (left). The
cord is held
neatly in place
by double-
sided adhesive
(right).

5. **Place your lamp where you want it and turn it on.**

   Easy breezy lemon parcheesi! Figure 14-4 highlights the full pizzazz of the finished fire truck.

FIGURE 14-4: The finished fire truck lamp is illustrious!

Mondrian Glass Pendant

Inspired by the work of modern abstract artist Piet Mondrian, this next upcycle is a real showstopper. The Mondrian glass pendant combines a stunning, stained-glass effect with impressive, cut wine bottles. The result is a truly magnificent light fixture. Figure 14-5 shows my Mondrian glass pendant.

FIGURE 14-5:
The beautiful, three-tiered chandelier made from cut wine bottles.

This light fixture features three upcycled wine bottles: green and blue bottles and one clear bottle I painted with a Mondrian, stained-glass effect. The stained-glass look makes the light truly spectacular — a modern piece of art that you can proudly display.

The first step to making a Mondrian glass pendant is collecting bottles that you like. Colorful glass bottles look great with light shining through.

You can tailor the look of this piece to your personal preference. Use primary or secondary colors. (Figure 14-6 shows the painting up close.) Or go the lo-fi route by skipping the paint job and using all colorful bottles instead.

FIGURE 14-6:
Mondrian-
inspired
pendant light.

You can make a post on social media asking friends to save the bottles you might be interested in. If you live in an apartment with communal recycling, you can put up a sign saying what you're looking for and provide a cardboard box for people to leave the bottles in.

You need to score, cut, sand, and de-goo (remove the labels) the wine bottles for this project using the steps laid out in Chapter 10.

A bottle cutter makes this a lot easier. Refer to Chapter 10, Figure 10-3 to see a bottle cutter in action.

With your bottles cut, smoothed, and cleaned you can add the Mondrian-stained glass effect. Gather your supplies before you get started:

>> ⅛" instant lead lines with adhesive backing

>> Liquid leading

>> Stained glass paint like Gallery Glass

>> A cutting board

>> A craft knife (such as an X-Acto) or paring knife

Use the following steps to apply the Mondrian-inspired pattern to your bottle:

1. **Create the Mondrian pattern by putting the peel-and-stick lead lining on the glass bottle using straight lines and right angles.**

   The top left of Figure 14-7 shows how this looks.

2. **Use liquid leading to join the gaps between your lead lines.**

   The top right of Figure 14-7 shows the gaps filled at the intersections of the lines with liquid leading. Let the leading dry completely overnight.

3. **After the liquid leading has dried, fill in the squares with the glass paint colors of your choice.**

   Mondrian style works with primary colors (red, blue, yellow) as well as black, white, and gray, but you can use any colors you like. The bottom left of Figure 14-7 shows the recently applied glass paint.

   Allow the paint to dry overnight.

4. **If you feel it's necessary, add a second coat of paint.**

   Hold the bottle up to a light to determine whether you've achieved the look you want. Some colors look more transparent than others. The bottom right of Figure 14-7 shows the dried look.

FIGURE 14-7:
Add lead lining shapes to your bottle (top left). The liquid leading connects the lead lines (top right). The stained-glass paint while wet (bottom left). This Mondrian glass bottle is now dry and ready to be hung as a light (bottom right).

5. Figure out the lengths you want your pendant cords to be.

Thread the pendant cord through the bottles (see the top of Figure 14-8). Then, hold the cord up to the ceiling to gauge your desired cord length. Mark it on the wire using a cable tie or a chalk mark.

TIP

It's helpful to have a friend assisting with this step. Ideally you should space the bottles so they aren't touching.

FIGURE 14-8: Gauging the length of wire for each pendant light requires holding them in place to see what height looks best for each bottle (top). The cords threaded and secured through the ceiling plate (bottom left). Stripping the wire of the pendant cords (bottom right).

6. **Thread the pendant cords through the pendant light ceiling plate and secure using the grommets that the light fixture comes with.**

   The bottom left of Figure 14-8 shows how this looks.

7. **Using either wire strippers, pliers, or scissors, make a shallow cut into the wire so that you can strip back the sheathing and reveal the black and white wires underneath.**

   The bottom right of Figure 14-8 shows this step.

8. **Connect the three lights by twisting together the wires according to color, as shown in the top of Figure 14-9.**

   It's essential to match the wires white to white, black to black. Never connect the black and white together as this can lead to an electrical fire.

   Secure with electrical tape, as shown in the bottom left of Figure 14-9.

9. **Turn off the power to the room at the breaker switch and connect the light to the outlet.**

   It's very important to turn off the power at the circuit breaker. Failing to do so can lead to severe electrical shock.

10. **Add the crossbar to the electrical cavity.**

    Doing so supports the weight of the pendant light.

11. **Connect the copper ground wire to the metal plate.**

    As shown in the bottom right of Figure 14-9.

12. **Connect the wires of the light to the power leads in the ceiling.**

    Connect the white wire of the lamp to the white ceiling wire, and the black lamp wire to the black ceiling wire. Twist the wires together and secure with marrettes, which are twist-on wire connectors.

TIP

    As a rule of thumb, black wires are hot, and white wires are neutral. If you're unsure, use a noncontact voltage detector from a hardware store. It will light up red when close to the hot wire.

13. **Mount the ceiling plate and secure it to the crossbar.**

14. **Add light bulbs to the fixture, turn the breaker back on, and switch your light on at the wall.**

    If the light doesn't switch on, recheck the connections of your wiring.

    Voila! Figure 14-10 shows the finished Mondrian glass pendant.

FIGURE 14-9:
Connecting
the three lights
(top). Close
up of the
connected
white wires
(bottom
left). The
neutral wire is
attached to the
metal crossbar
to ground
the circuit
(bottom right).

FIGURE 14-10:
The finished
result of the
three bottles
hung together
is absolutely
gorgeous.

Chapter **15**

Upcycling Art for Any Space

Upcycling and art go hand in hand. Upcycling is all about creatively reusing waste, and art is the perfect vehicle. Creating upcycled art just makes sense. The materials are abundant, and the possibilities are endless.

In this chapter, I show you how to use two upcycled art techniques: mosaic and collage. The first art upcycle is a dramatically gorgeous beach plastic mosaic. This piece uses found plastic to highlight the problematic abundance of beach litter. This art makes a profound environmental statement.

The second art upcycle features the collage technique, an absolute classic. Collage art has been around since the dawn of paper (around 200 BC), and it still hasn't gone out of style. Collages are timeless. They're also the perfect medium for conveying a mood, message, or an overall appreciation for beauty.

Beach Plastic Mosaic

Surfer and eco content creator Reyanne Mustafa made the gorgeous beach plastic mosaic in Figure 15-1. Reyanne was inspired to upcycle the seemingly endless kids' plastic toys littered on the beach after summer. This piece is called *Endless (Warming) Summer*. In a visual nod to the movie poster for *The Endless Summer*, the art illustrates the alarming reality of beach plastic.

Doing a beach cleanup is a fabulous way to find plastic for upcycling. There's plenty to be discovered – lots of beach toys crack and split and are ultimately abandoned. Upcycling found beach plastic does double duty. First, it saves marine animals from eating it, and second, it finds a use for something that can take more than 450 years to decompose.

Figure 15-2 shows some of the beach plastic that Reyanne found.

1. **Source a board to upcycle for the back of your art piece and cut it into a circle.**

   You can use plywood or even a cardboard box. Reyanne found her board in the alley behind her house.

FIGURE 15-2: Here's some reclaimed plastic for the blue section.

2. **Paint the background of your mosaic to make it easy to know where to glue which color.**

   After your paint dries, you can practice placing the plastic on top of the board so you can visualize where it will go. Figure 15-3 shows this step.

TIP

3. **Cut the plastic into smaller pieces using scissors.**

   Figure 15-4 shows the ideal size for this.

   Using a different bin for each color organizes the pieces and keeps them contained.

TIP

4. **Use upcycled Styrofoam for the foam of the waves.**

5. **Glue the pieces on top of the corresponding background color.**

   This step is arguably the most fun. Using a hot glue gun works well. Figure 15-5 illustrates the desired effect.

FIGURE 15-4:
Here's a
close-up of
the cut pieces,
which shows
their ideal size.

FIGURE 15-5:
Gluing the
pieces to the
background
completes
this gorgeous
mosaic.

The Classic Collage

A magazine cut-out collage is the quintessential upcycled art piece. It's a fantastic way to use up leftover magazines, old and dishevelled books, and whatever other bits and bobs speak to you. Don't be shy about expressing yourself!

Figure 15-6 shows a collage made with a printed photograph and magazine cutouts.

FIGURE 15-6:
Collages are a great way to combine materials that speak to you.

To make a collage, gather materials like paper, magazines, newspapers, old books, and little found objects that you've been saving.

TIP

Looking for materials? Ask your hair salon if they have any old magazines.

1. Start by cutting out images that you like.

   When it comes to collage, there aren't a lot of rules. Figure 15-7 shows a printed photograph being cut for use.

FIGURE 15-7:
Begin by cutting up images that appeal to you.

2. **(optional) Use a precision craft knife (often used for scrapbooking) to cut out small areas.**

   Figure 15-8 shows the intricate cuts you can make with this tool.

FIGURE 15-8:
Precision craft
knives are
great for
cutting out
small areas.

3. **Arrange the cutouts on your chosen background to visualize the piece as it unfolds.**

   Figure 15-9 shows this step.

4. **Once you like the feel of the collage, use a foam paintbrush to apply a few key points of glue to the back of the cutouts to secure them in place. Then press them onto your background.**

   A decoupage glue like Mod Podge works well.

5. **Let your glued images dry for a few minutes, and then thinly and evenly apply a coat of decoupage glue on top of the collage.**

   This topcoat seals and protects the piece. Figure 15-10 shows the freshly applied decoupage glue.

FIGURE 15-9:
Playing around
with the
cutouts on the
background is
helpful.

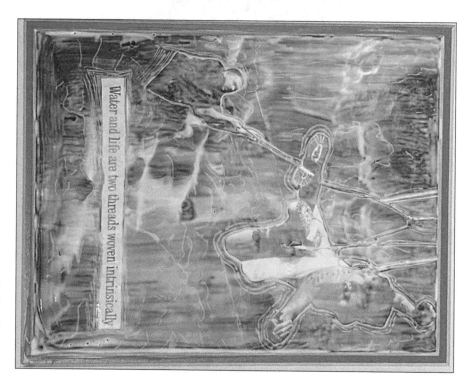

FIGURE 15-10:
Using
decoupage
glue as a
topcoat
protects your
collage from
tearing.

6. **After allowing your collage to fully dry, you can frame it.**

Upcycling a thrift store frame is the perfect way to elevate the look of your art piece. Figure 15-11 shows the framed collage.

FIGURE 15-11:
Using a thrift
store frame is
a great way to
frame artwork
for less.

Chapter **16**
Planters on Cloud Wine

Wine and plant lovers, this chapter is for you! Get ready to add a splash of green to your life with two vino-inspired planters. These upcycles are fab, because they use readily available materials: wine corks and bottles. You can find both easily. Ask a friend or at your local restaurant, or look for these materials peeking out of your curbside recycling bins — they're begging you to wash and repurpose them!

In this chapter, I show you how to make both wine cork and wine bottle planters. Both upcycles are ideal for people who don't have a natural green thumb. The wine cork planters are made with succulent clippings. Succulents are gorgeous, and they're wonderfully hardy — meaning it takes some effort to kill them. Does that sound like a fit for you? Then you'll also love the wine bottle planters that have a handy self-watering feature. They're perfect for people who forget to water their plants or travel a lot. Your garden will be on cloud wine.

Constructing Wine Cork Planters

Wine cork planters are magnetic and really dress up your fridge. They also make for lovely little gifts. If you're having a special bottle of wine, be sure to set the cork aside to make a special memento in the form of a succulent cork planter.

These planters are simple to make and require only wine corks, magnets, some soil, and succulent clippings. The tools you need are:

>> Hot glue gun

>> Paring knife

>> Spoon

>> Screwdriver

Once you have your materials, follow these steps:

1. **Use the head of a screwdriver to punch a hole in the top of the cork.**

   Figure 16-1 shows how this should look.

FIGURE 16-1:
Making a hole
in the cork with
a screwdriver.

2. **Place the paring knife into the hole and rotate it in a circle to carve out a hole.**

Your hole should go about halfway down the cork. Figure 16-2 shows the technique.

TIP

Working over a box or a newspaper is a great way to contain the cork shavings.

FIGURE 16-2:
Carving a hole into the cork with a paring knife.

3. **Glue magnets onto your corks with a hot glue gun.**

Figure 16-3 features the tools and materials to use for this.

4. **Take a spoon and fill your mini cork planters with soil.**

You might want to use your fingertip to push the soil down. Figure 16-4 demonstrates what the soil looks like in the cork planter holes.

TIP

Adding another magnet to the outside of the box will make it easy to keep the corks upright as you fill them with soil.

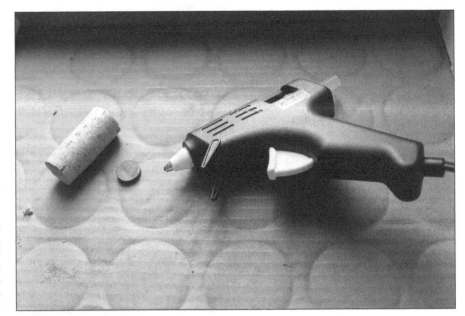

FIGURE 16-3:
Adding the
magnet to
the cork turns
this upcycle
into fridge
decor.

FIGURE 16-4:
Putting soil
into the corks
with a spoon.

5. **Plant your succulent clippings into the cork planters by poking the clippings into the soil and packing more soil on top to keep them in place.**

   Figure 16-5 displays how this looks.

FIGURE 16-5: The succulent clippings are now in the cork planters.

6. **Admire your new cork planters on the fridge!**

   Figure 16-6 presents the finished result.

FIGURE 16-6:
Placing the
cork planters
on the fridge
completes
the look.

Cutting Wine Bottle Planters

Wine bottle planters are a stylish way to reuse glass wine bottles. The best part is that they're self-watering!

To make a planter you need a cut wine bottle. Please refer to Chapter 10 for the techniques on how to cut wine bottles.

This project requires:

TIP

» Adhesive remover

Try using lighter fluid or make a natural adhesive remover with equal parts baking soda and coconut oil.

» Landscaping fabric

» Oil burner wicks/string

» Potted plant or herb with soil

» Hot water in a pot/bucket

» 60-grit waterproof sandpaper

» Butter knife

» Paring knife

» Glue

1. **Following the directions in Chapter 10, cut a wine bottle.**

   Refer to Figure 16-7 for how the cut bottle should look.

FIGURE 16-7: This cut wine bottle is ready to be transformed into a planter.

2. **Sand the cut edges of the wine bottle smooth using 60-grit waterproof sandpaper.**

    Figure 16-8 demonstrates this.

3. **Soak the bottle in hot water for 15–20 minutes to loosen the label for removal.**

    Figure 16-9 shows this step.

TIP

It's more efficient to remove the labels *after* you cut the bottles because some bottles will break during cutting.

4. **Scrape off the softened label with a butter knife.**

    Figure 16-10 shows how using an adhesive remover eliminates the last stubborn bits of the label.

5. **Cut a piece of landscaping fabric into a 3"-4" square.**

6. **Fold the top corner to make a triangle.**

FIGURE 16-9:
Soaking the bottle makes it easier to remove the label.

FIGURE 16-10:
An adhesive remover makes removing the label a piece of cake.

7. Place a dab of glue to secure the fold.

8. Pierce a slit into the tip of the cone with a paring knife.

9. Insert the wick into the landscaping fabric cone.

10. Place the cone wick combo into the top of the wine bottle.

Figure 16-11 shows steps 5–10.

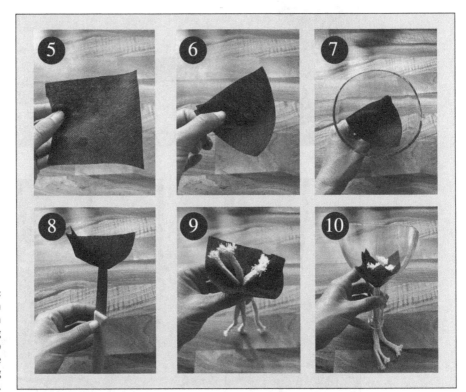

FIGURE 16-11:
Making a cone with landscaping fabric to secure the self-watering wick.

11. Fill the top of the bottle with a plant and add water to the bottom to complete the project!

Figure 16-12 shows the final look.

FIGURE 16-12: Admiring the completed wine bottle planter.

5

The Four Ps of Selling Your Pieces

IN THIS PART . . .

Find out how to how to style, stage, and photograph your creations like a pro.

Discover how to gear up for a shoot and create the most flattering angle and lighting setups.

Take the guesswork out of pricing so that you can flip your pieces for a profit.

Uncover where to post and how to create an online presence to promote and sell your pieces.

Chapter **17**

Planning for Props and Photography

When it comes to the home decor world, great photos will make or break you. Think about it: You can create the most gorgeous pieces, but if you don't take solid photos, no one will realize the beauty.

If you're interested in selling your upcycled pieces, this will be one of the most important chapters for you. Creating high-quality photos of your work is essential for gaining customers. You want to take inviting pictures so viewers think, "Oh, that would look phenomenal in my home!"

In this chapter, you'll find out how to style and stage upcycled photo shoots. You'll also discover where and how to take the best photos, with simple and effective tips that elevate your pictures to the next level.

Setting the Scene with Styling and Staging

After investing time and money to create beautiful pieces, it's important to shoot photos that really make them shine. This is what bona fide styling and staging can do.

Setting the mood with props

Props add color, texture, and visual intrigue, and they enhance the overall look of your upcycles. The props help to evoke a mood. They prompt the viewer to imagine how incredible their life would be with that piece.

Here are some tips for working with props:

>> **Plants add vibrance.** Plants, flowers, and greenery bring your image to life. Work with plants to add extra oomph. Figure 17-1 shows the impact of using flowers in your shoot.

FIGURE 17-1:
The roses contribute to the romantic mood of this vignette.

TIP

>> **Match the style and era.** The props should complement one another and the item they're showcasing. Figure 17-2 shows how the jewelry highlights the vintage style of this tiered organizer.

Thrift stores are great for sourcing incredible props, like old books, glassware, and vintage suitcases.

FIGURE 17-2:
The props you pick should have the same vibe as the item they're paired with.

>> **Enhance without going overboard.** A few props are great, but too many make the scene look cluttered. Figure 17-3 is an example of what *not* to do. This scene is a hot mess.

What not to do.

FIGURE 17-3:
Too many
props and
a scattered
background
make this shot
feel busy.

>> **Work with color.** The color wheel is your friend and offers lots of options. You can work with a monochromatic palette, using a repeating color with different shades, or you can work with complementary colors on opposite sides of the color wheel (for example, pairing yellow and purple). For a soothing effect, choose colors that are next to each other on the color wheel. This is an analogous combination. Refer to Chapter 3 for more information about color wheels.

>> **Texture adds charm.** Texture attracts attention and adds character. Think about the mood you're trying to convey and the texture(s) that would heighten that. This could mean including wood, textiles, glass, or metal.

Location, location, location

Where you shoot matters. The location you choose has a huge impact on how the photos will look. Shooting by a source of natural light, like a bright window is ideal. Figure 17-4 was taken right by a window.

FIGURE 17-4:
Natural light
makes this
upcycled
dessert tower
glimmer and
gleam.

Creating the ideal background is key to establishing the atmosphere. Make sure that the area you're capturing is presentable. Anything messy or cluttered detracts from your photos.

Brick or whitewashed wood offers fabulous background texture. Figure 17-5 shows the beautiful interplay between a piece of art and the whitewashed wall behind it.

FIGURE 17-5: These whitewashed walls are the perfect complementary backdrop to this gorgeous art by Paddy Meade.

Change up your backdrop by ordering vinyl photography backdrops online from Etsy. This is a great hack to bringing different textures like stone, marble, brick, and wood into your shoots.

Wooden floors are another great way to include a textured backdrop. This is especially impactful when shooting small, home decor items. Figure 17-6 presents a jewelry tower offset against a wooden floor.

Photographing like a Pro

Now that you're set for staging, it's time to talk about gear. Because you need to shoot with something!

Gearing up for a shoot

A good DSLR camera is lovely, but don't be discouraged if you don't own one. You can take fabulous photos on an iPhone and Android phone, too. It's better to start with what you have and invest in more sophisticated equipment as your business grows.

TIP

Using Portrait mode on a mobile phone camera app blurs out the background. It's a reliable way to make your subject pop!

TIP

If you have a DSLR, shoot in manual mode so that you can adjust the aperture and shutter speed and influence the exposure.

Slower shutter speeds mean the eye of the camera is open longer. This allows more light in, but also opens up the possibility of the dreaded blurry pic. Figure 17-7 highlights an image that was ruined because of camera shake. You can avoid blurry images by shooting on a tripod, which keeps your camera steady so your photos will be sharp and focused.

FIGURE 17-7:
The top of this dessert tower image is blurry because this image was taken without the steadying influence of a tripod.

Finding the best angle

People aren't the only photo subjects that have flattering sides. Highlighting angles in furniture and home decor makes your images look intriguing.

Figure 17-8 shows that while furniture face-on looks a bit chunky, angles are chic. Try a few setups to find the most appealing angles.

FIGURE 17-8:
Face-on is
heavy (left),
whereas angles
highlight the
bones of a
piece (right).

Photo composition

Composition is the art of arranging. It's the way that the elements of the image are placed within the shot. Good composition is balanced, although it may or may not be symmetrical.

Here are some important factors to consider for composition.

- » **Focal point:** The focal point is the first thing people will see when they look at your photo. It's the main subject of the image. In this case, you want your item to be the focal point.

- » **Be mindful about what's in frame:** This includes anything visible in the photograph. Be conscious about what's in the space around your main subject and what's in the background.

- » **The rule of thirds:** This classic method of composition divides the frame into thirds with both horizontal and vertical lines. This results in a grid with nine equal squares. According to this rule, the most visually interesting images use the crosshairs of one of the power points (shown in orange in Figure 17-9) as the focal point for the image.

TIP

Look for a setting on your camera to overlay a grid when shooting. This can be helpful when you first start composing images with the rule of thirds.

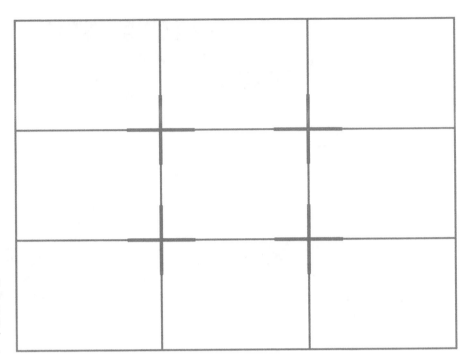

FIGURE 17-9:
The orange
power points
are ideal places
to use as your
focal point.

TIP

As a basic rule of thumb, furniture and home decor look best when you shoot them at eye level.

TIP

For more information, search for the article "10 Tips for Taking Better Photos" at Dummies.com.

Using natural and fill lighting

Natural light is best. Shoot by a window and observe where the light falls and what is in shadows.

If you're getting silhouettes on your subject, it could be due to backlighting or side lighting. This is when the light falls behind or next to your subject, casting shadows. Figure 17-10 shows the difference between front lighting and side lighting. It's not wrong or right, but definitely a creative choice.

Here are some options for supplementing your lighting:

>> **Reflector:** Inexpensive and versatile. You can use this reflective surface for bouncing natural and artificial light. It folds down to a small size.

FIGURE 17-10:
See the
difference
between front
lighting
(left) and side
lighting (right).

>> **Clamp light:** Can be positioned at a 90-degree angle away from the subject. You can attach it to a tripod in a pinch.

>> **Ambient light:** Indirect light that offers a moody vibe.

>> **Ring light:** Creates soft, dimmable light. The light of choice of beauty vloggers.

>> **Softbox:** Creates diffused light because the bulb is enclosed by a box that softens it, hence the name.

>> **LED light panel:** Offers great directional light to use as a primo side light. These panels are efficient and durable, especially when compared to glass bulbs.

Accenting images through editing

Editing images is what makes them spectacular! A raw, unedited image is like wearing a good outfit without confidence. The elements are there, but it lacks luster.

TIP

Play around with editing to see the impact each change can make.

Editing tools

The native photo apps on your phone and computer allow you to tweak brightness, contrast, highlights, shadows, vibrance, saturation and, if you're lucky, vignette.

You can upgrade your capability by using professional software like Adobe Lightroom (entry level) and Adobe Photoshop (more complex). The image on the top of Figure 17-11 shows a raw photo as it was shot, and the bottom image is the same photo after I edited it using Adobe Lightroom.

FIGURE 17-11:
The photo before editing (top). The same photo after editing in Adobe Lightroom (bottom).

TIP

It's easy to use Adobe Lightroom to adjust the brightness and remove shadows in the image. You can also adjust the color and tone of the image and rotate it if you need to straighten it. For more information, consider reading *Adobe Photoshop Lightroom Classic for Dummies* by Rob Sylvan (John Wiley & Sons, Inc.).

TIP

Adobe Creative Cloud currently offers a plan with both Adobe Lightroom and Photoshop for $9.99 (U.S.) monthly, which is a great price for this professional software.

Presets

A series of saved edits on Adobe Lightroom is called a *preset*. You can use Adobe presets to perform a bunch of edits in one go with just a single click.

TIP

You can also save the edits you've done on another image as a preset. This is handy if you want to do the same edits to multiple images.

TIP

Many bloggers sell packs of presets that you can buy and install in Lightroom. If you like a certain blogger's styles, consider purchasing their presets. It's an effective way to get their look, for way less time!

Chapter **18**

Putting Together Pricing and Promotion

Figuring out what to charge for your furniture can be tricky. When you begin flipping furniture, it may feel uncomfortable to put a value on your work Please hear this: You deserve to make a profit! Upcycling furniture is a valuable service, and it takes time, energy, and supplies.

Like any item, the local supply and demand influence the price you can charge. Factors like the complexity of your techniques, the market demands, the competition's offerings, and your reputation as an upcycler all come into play. In this chapter, I suggest factors to consider when pricing, and share a handy-dandy furniture pricing calculator that takes out the guesswork.

Once you've nailed down pricing, the next step is figuring out *where* and *how* to sell. No need to stress — this chapter covers that, too. Find out how to attract your ideal customers like bees to blooms!

Pricing Your Piece

When you're just starting out, it's normal to be clueless about how to price your pieces. Without guidance, it can be difficult to figure out what an item is worth, and what someone would pay for it. Let's simplify the process so that you can maximize your profits.

Flipping for profit

When it comes to pricing, you have a few factors to consider:

>> How much you paid for the furniture

>> The cost of the supplies/materials used while upcycling

>> How much time you spent on it

>> How much markup/profit you want to make

TIP

The best way to keep your costs down and profits up is to find free or inexpensive items to upcycle. Items under $50 are ideal, but don't sacrifice quality for price. Remember, anything that you have to spend a lot of time fixing also increases the time and expense of your project.

TIP

Keep track of all the expenses associated with your upcycle — for instance, the cost of the supplies used and other overheads like gas for picking up the furniture.

Using the handy-dandy furniture pricing calculator

The basic formula for pricing is

Price = (total costs) × (markup)

Let's go through the specifics:

>> Total costs = (furniture cost) + (supplies)

>> Furniture cost = the price you paid for the item

>> Supplies = the cost of the supplies used for *this* project

Table 18-1 shows how to figure out what your associated expenses were by factoring in the overall costs and the percentage used *on this project specifically*.

>> The markup is where you make the profit. Use a percentage of your total cost, such as 200 percent, and then adjust according to how much time you spent and importantly, what you think your market will pay. Read more about this in the "Purposeful pricing" section.

TABLE 18-1   **Project Expenses**

Expense	Total Cost	Percentage Used	Cost for Project
Coffee table	$50	100%	$50
Sandpaper	$6	100%	$6
Primer	$14	50%	$7
Paint	$40	50%	$20
Paintbrush	$25	Reuse for 10+ projects (brushes can last for years if you treat them right!)	$2.50
Sealant	$36	25%	$9
Hardware	$8	100%	$8
Gas	$60	12.5%	$7.50
Total cost:	$239		$110

Purposeful pricing

When it comes to pricing anything, consider supply and demand. Here are a few factors that influence the price you should charge for your upcycled furniture:

>> **Location, location, location:** The market you're selling to (also known as where you live) has a huge influence on the price you can command. The demand for home decor in cities is way higher than in rural areas, and customers tend to pay more per item because they have more disposable income. Will people in your area pay $220 for a coffee table?

>> **The competition:** Before pricing your item, check out what your competitors are charging. This gives you a solid feel for the market.

TIP

Here's a spy-level hack to figure out how much the competition are *actually* selling their items for. On Facebook Marketplace, you have the option to "save listing" by clicking the icon in the listing that looks like a tag. You can then easily track how long it takes to sell the item and if the price is reduced along the way. Follow a few items to get a good understanding of the local demand. Figure 18-1 shows where this feature is.

FIGURE 18-1:
The "save listing" feature on Facebook Marketplace keeps you updated on a listing.

REMEMBER

When comparing your piece with the competitors, factor in the style, size, and amount of refinishing that went into yours versus theirs. This leads me to the next point. . .

>> **The complexity of the upcycle:** Generally speaking, you can ask a higher price for using more complex techniques. For instance, you can charge more for a coffee table you painted with a three-color layer technique and added patina (read more in Chapter 7) than your competitor does for a coffee table painted with only one color and technique.

REMEMBER

You can always reduce the price of your item if it isn't selling, but you can't ask for more than your listing price. If you get a lot of hits quickly, you've priced too low.

>> **What the market wants:** Having a clear understanding of what pieces your market is hot for is a gamechanger. Unique pieces stand out and garner attention, but neutral pieces look great in most homes and often sell more quickly.

TIP

Experiment with different styles and techniques to find the happy place where you can make lots of sales but also express yourself creatively.

>> **Your reputation:** Your notoriety influences the amount someone is willing to pay for your work. Just like with artists, people pay more for pieces from reputable upcyclers.

TIP

As you build up your following, you will be able to bump up your prices and sell items faster.

Making the highest margins

>> **Buy low, sell high:** Free pieces can offer the highest return. Don't turn up your nose at a valuable score from a curbside or friend.

>> **Start with quality pieces:** It's hard to repair pieces with wonky drawers, and it takes a lot of time. Scratches and dings are okay, but avoid buying pieces that have major structural damage.

>> **Real wood, real value:** Solid wooden furniture with dovetail joints (when wood is interlocked like a zipper) stand the test of time and are appealing to customers. A maker's stamp on the piece is also a great indication of quality.

>> **Selectively replace hardware:** New hardware adds up, and it's not always necessary to replace it. If the item has all the hardware intact, consider reusing it, or save it for another upcycle.

>> **Practice makes you more productive:** Time and practice sharpen your skills and shorten your time to flip furniture, meaning higher profits.

>> **Offer paid delivery:** This is a great way to make a bit more cash and upsell your services. It also removes a potential barrier to purchasing that some buyers might have.

>> **Stay on trend:** Give the people what they want by knowing the trendy colors and styles. For instance, adding hairpin legs to a drawer can turn it into a trendy mid-century modern-style side table.

TIP

Consider working on multiple pieces at once to save time and efficiently use your supplies. You can paint another piece while your first one is drying.

Posting and Promoting

These days when people are searching for furniture, they like to do it from the comfort of their own home. Show up where your customers are and post your items online.

Creating an online presence

A valuable thing about building an online presence is that you don't need to invest too much to begin. You can find many impactful places to sell, and they are mostly free!

The best way to appeal to your customers is to know who they are, where they are, and what they're looking for.

Make a buyer persona of your ideal customer. This is a fictionalized bio of your customer that includes their name, age, interests, income — essentially who they are. With this person in mind, it gets easier to understand your customers' needs and expectations.

Finding places to sell your upcycles

It's easy and accessible to reach a broad market for your upcycled furniture online. Here are some of the best places to sell your pieces:

>> **Facebook Marketplace:** This is the current leader in the market for buying and selling. The sheer volume of local buyers that you gain access to is incredible; especially given that this platform is free to use. It's also helpful to put a face to the name of potential buyers.

>> **Instagram:** This is a visual platform that's highly effective for sales. Local customers can comment on your posts and stories to claim a piece, and you can message them directly to finalize sales.

>> **Home decor buy and sell groups on Facebook:** These are awesome for creating a solid reputation for yourself within the local community because past customers can comment on your posts, which acts as a strong referral for new customers.

>> **Online classifieds like Craigslist:** This is the OG classic for online sales. It's no frills, but it's simple to use and allows you to easily reach local buyers.

>> **Boutiques/antique stores that sell upcycled furniture:** These are the perfect places to reach a niche audience. These stores take a percentage of your sales, but their customers are often willing to pay higher prices.

>> **eBay:** This site reaches millions of shoppers online. Appeal to shoppers in your area by advertising "Local Pickup Only."

>> **Your own website:** This is a great way to showcase your work.

>> **YouTube:** Having a YouTube channel where you show off your work can be a powerful traffic driver for gaining a following and sending traffic to your website.

To increase your chances of being seen, post in multiple places at once.

Selling with sizzle: Helpful selling tips

When it comes to selling your furniture, price and location aren't the only factors. There's also *how* you sell.

Keep these considerations in mind:

>> **Photography:** The staging, photography, and lighting have a huge impact on the perceived value of your piece. That's why I cover them extensively in Chapter 17. *Cough* Don't skip this step. *Cough*

>> **Descriptive ad copy:** Size matters. Make sure to include all the dimensions in your listings so people don't have to ask for them. Also use keywords to pop up in search results, such as *farmhouse, rustic,* and *reclaimed wood look.*

>> **Hook 'em and reel 'em:** Everyone loves a good story. Engage your audience by sharing an intriguing tidbit about the piece or suggested ways that they could use it. If you can get your customers to visualize using the item in their home, they're more likely to consider buying it. Here's an example: "With a tray and your favorite stemware, this gorgeous cart would make a perfect at-home bar. Can you imagine it in your living room?!"

>> **Stay in touch:** Encourage customers to follow you on social media, and follow them back. You can ask them to send you a picture of their furniture in its new home and post the pic and tag them. They'll often comment on the post saying how much they love the piece, which encourages new buyers. Also follow up with them in a few months to see if there's anything else they're looking for. Repeat customers are the best customers!

6

The Part of Tens

Know what gems to look out for while you're thrift shopping.

Discover some fun and effective ways to repurpose glass jars.

Chapter **19**

Ten Things to Look for at a Thrift Store

Thrift stores are treasure troves for upcyclers! In this chapter, I share the ten things that are always worth looking out for.

Real Wood Furniture Pieces

Older furniture is often of a higher quality than furniture made today. Items like dressers and velvet chairs retain their value and are ideal for upcycling.

Figure 19-1 shows a stunning velvet armchair for sale at a thrift store.

TIP

Keep an eye out for American or Dutch-made furniture. You can easily resell it for a tidy profit *without doing a thing to it*!

Vintage Glassware

There is often incredible, vintage glassware available at thrift stores. Glassware objects range from stunning crystal pieces and milk glass to Depression glass and quirky retro glassware. These perfect thrift store scores are easy to clean and upcycle into home decor or to resell as sets.

If you're looking to resell glassware, keep an eye out for:

» Sets of four or six glasses

» Retro barware and *Mad Men*–era cocktail glasses

>> Milk glass

>> Depression glass

>> Jadeite

>> Glass jugs and bottles

>> Vintage Pyrex

>> Crystal glassware

Figure 19-2 shows a lovely selection of crystal glassware for sale.

FIGURE 19-2:
You'll find lots
of great crystal
glassware at
thrift stores.

TIP

Look for the especially valuable jadeite markings of Anchor Hocking Fire King (*Fire-King*), McKee (*Mck*), and Jeanette (*J*) glass companies. Vintage McKee and Jeannette jadeite will glow when exposed to UV/blacklight flashlights because these dishes were made with uranium prior to WWII.

Figure 19-3 shows some beautiful jadeite salt and pepper shakers.

GLASSWARE STYLES

When you're scouring thrift stores or estate sales for items to upcycle, keep an eye out for the following styles of glass:

- **Milk glass:** This white, opaque glass was porcelain for the masses. It was popular in both America and England from 1835 until the 1980s.

- **Depression glass:** This raised-pattern glassware was mass-produced from 1920 through 1950 in virtually every color. It was created to bring affordable glassware to working class Americans during the Depression — hence the name.

- **Jadeite:** Jadeite is opaque glass with a mint green hue. This popular dishware from the 1930s is now a highly sought-after collectible.

FIGURE 19-3: Keep an eye out for vintage jadeite with a mint green hue.

Lamps

Thrift stores are the perfect place to find beautiful lighting. Pay more attention to the bases specifically, because it's quite easy to swap out the lamp shades. Also, be sure to test the lamps at an outlet in the store prior to purchase to make sure that they work.

TIP

Don't like the color? Spray paint the base of a thrifted lamp to completely revamp the look!

Vases

Thrift stores have *tons* of great vases, so there's no reason to buy one new. Also, vases make great succulent terrariums!

Artwork

Although some thrift store artwork is truly horrific, other pieces are uniquely stunning. It's also worth looking at the frames because thrifting is a great way to find quality frames for less.

TIP

You can repurpose frames into chalkboards or jewelry displays.

Thrifted art is great for repurposing. You can paint over the canvas to create your own unique artwork, which is way cheaper than buying large canvases new. Bonus points if you like the frame that it comes in, as custom framing is quite expensive.

TIP

Figure 19-4 shows a selection of artwork available at a thrift shop.

FIGURE 19-4:
Some artwork
and frames
ready to be
upcycled.

Wicker

Wicker items like baskets and furniture are timeless. As a bonus, they're also easy to wipe clean. So, if you see some in good condition, be sure to pick them up!

Textiles

You can find high-quality blankets, comforters, curtains, tablecloths, sheets, and pillows at thrift stores. Yes, of course, you'll have to wash them, but that shouldn't deter you. Most people overlook this section, but if you're diligent, you can often find lovely vintage textiles up for grabs. You can also creatively repurpose them as upholstery.

Old Books

Old books look great for styling. Take off the covers and use them to decorate a shelf or for staging. It's a great way to add color and character to a piece that you're selling.

Figure 19-5 shows how effective books can be for styling upcycled photo shoots.

FIGURE 19-5:
Vintage books really pop for staging!

TIP

Keep an eye out for first edition books. These are from the first-ever printing of a book and can be quite valuable. The copyright page will say "first edition" or "first printing."

Silverware

Real silver might be hiding amongst the cutlery at thrift stores. Look for tarnished pieces and polish them up at home. Silverware has a great resale value, and it can be upcycled in many unique and creative ways. It's perfect for making garden ornaments or markers, hooks and cabinets handles, windchimes and jewelry — the possibilities are endless!

TIP

Look out for indented marks on silver to discover where and when it was made, what it's made of and who made it. Sterling silver is made of at least 92.5 percent silver and will often be marked with *sterling*, *92.5*, or *925*.

Seasonal Decor

Just before or after the holidays is the perfect time to find epic seasonal decor. There's no need to buy new; you can thrift amazing vintage and one-of-a-kind seasonal items. Keep your eyes peeled in the off-season, too; you never know when it might be Christmas in July!

Chapter **20**

Ten Ways to Reuse Glass Jars

G lass jars are like the Swiss Army knife of the upcycling world — you can reuse them in countless ways. In this chapter, I share ten clever ways to repurpose them. Once you start upcycling glass jars, you won't want to stop, which is great because there are about a jillion of them in the world. You likely already have some in your home or recycling bin!

Vases

Using jars as vases is pretty sweet. Position mason jars as vases for table center-pieces, or hang lots of little ones with flowers for a touch of whimsy. Figure 20-1 shows how to repurpose baby jars into delightful hanging vases.

FIGURE 20-1:
Hanging flower
jars are lovely.

Candles

Add an instant vibe with glass jar candles. You can work them in a few ways:

>> Hand-pour soy wax candles. (Read about the method for this in Chapter 13.)

>> Paint the jar and add a tealight inside.

>> Add a tealight and suspend the jar with a string to make a hanging lantern. The glass really adds a touch of class!

>> Wrap ribbon around the jar for a textured glow, as shown in Figure 20-2.

Gift Jars

Everyone loves receiving gifts in jars! For a thoughtful present, layer in the dry ingredients of a cookie mix. You can include the baking instructions on a gift tag. Then, top the jar with a piece of upcycled fabric and some twine, as shown in Figure 20-3. Or, make a hot chocolate mix in a jar with cocoa powder and marshmallows. For bonus points, attach a candy cane to the side.

FIGURE 20-3:
Homemade
cookie jars are
sure to be well
received.

Animal Jars

One fun way to dress up storage jars is to collect and clean out some jars and then super glue an animal toy onto the lid. Allow the glue to dry, and then spray paint the lids your favorite color. Figure 20-4 shows some animal jars being used to hold cotton balls and Q-tips.

FIGURE 20-4:
Animal jars
by Audrey
Kuether of Oh
So Lovely.

Mason Jar Oil Lamp

DIY oil lamps are an exquisite way to add ambience, especially during the holidays. To make an oil lamp, add olive oil, essential oils, and beautiful botanicals to a mason jar and top it with a floating wick. The left side of Figure 20-5 shows a gorgeous oil lamp made by Patti Estep of Hearth and Vine.

TIP

To make sure your botanicals stay submerged, use a mixture of small and large natural elements like cinnamon sticks, pinecones, cedar branches, and dried orange slices.

TIP

To find floating wicks, search for *large round floating wicks* on Amazon.

Herb Garden

This indoor herb garden is a stunning way to keep fresh herbs. To re-create this idea, attach pipe clamps to a board. (You can find pipe clamps in the plumbing section of your hardware store.) Then add rocks, soil, and a herb plant to a mason jar and place it within the adjustable pipe clamps. The right side of Figure 20-5 illustrates the look.

FIGURE 20-5:
These oil lamps from Patti Estep of Hearth and Vine are a beautiful way to add natural elements to your decor (left). Chrissy Creaser of Sandpiper Woodworking made this indoor herb garden (right).

Food Storage

Glass jars are perfect for preserves like jams and pickles and for bulk food storage. Figure 20-6 displays a pantry to be proud of.

TIP

For a cohesive look, collect multiples of the same type of jar or find jars of the same height.

TIP

It's helpful to label the jars so that you remember what's in each one.

FIGURE 20-6:
Glass jars are perfect for bulk food storage.

Bird Feeder

Upcycled bird feeders are attractive to birds and humans alike. The left side of Figure 20-7 shows a charming bird feeder made with a mason jar and topped with vintage dinner plates. It's a fantastic way to invite aviary friends to your garden or patio!

FIGURE 20-7:
Mason jar bird
feeder by Hal
Malmquist of
BirdFeeders
Rus.com (left).
This dramatic
mason jar
chandelier
from Jeff
Risinger and
Mark Winn of
BootsNGus.
com is the
epitome of
farmhouse
chic (right).

Mason Jar Chandelier

A cluster of mason jars with pendant lights makes for an extraordinary chandelier. Add holes to the lids so that the heat from the bulb can safely disperse. The right side of Figure 20-7 displays a gorgeous light fixture by Jeff Risinger and Mark Winn of BootsNGus.com.

TIP

Use a mixture of antique blue and clear quart-sized mason jars for a striking combination.

Seasonal Luminaries

Luminaries are a gorgeous addition to any holiday decor. Figure 20-8 shows a fun idea for Halloween. Fill a jar with fake spider webs, a plastic spider, and a battery-operated tealight for instant ambience.

FIGURE 20-8:
DIY luminaries
are easy to
make and look
fabulous!

Index

A

acrylic paint, 61

acrylic-alkyd paint, 62

adhesive wallpaper, 69–71

Adobe Lightroom, 246–247

aging wood with tea, vinegar, and steel wool, 87–91

alkyd paint, 62

ambient light, 244

Amin, Rumman, 46

analogous color scheme, 44

Anderson, Kate, 13

angles, in photography, 242–243

animal jars, 270

antique items, defined, 32

antique stores, selling items at, 254

armchair, Victorian-style, 177–179

Armstrong, Claire, 14, 69

artwork

  beach plastic mosaic, 212–215

  buying at thrift stores, 263–264

  collage, 216–220

  overview, 211

  upcycling inspiration, 17–19

Asbury, Sonny, 139

At Charlotte's House, 12

B

background for photos, 240

bar, steamer trunk

  glass door, creating, 168–169

  hairpin legs, adding, 171–172

  overview, 165–166

  plywood frame, inserting, 170

  plywood frame, making, 167–168

  supplies for, 166

bathroom vanity, 12

batting, 121

beach plastic mosaic, 212–215

bed bugs, inspecting for, 34

beeswax bar, 96

Behn, Sally, 139

Benjamin Moore Color Viewer tool, 45–46

bird feeders, 272–273

BirdFeeders Rus.com, 273

black marks, removing, 110

Blair, Carlene, 20

bleeding through, 55

block pallets, 147

books, buying at thrift stores, 265–266

boot bench, 17–18

BootsNGus.com, 14–16, 273

bottles, glass

  cutting, 134–136

  drilling holes into, 140–142

  labels, removing, 137–138

  Mondrian glass pendant, 203–210

  overview, 133

  planters, 226–232

  sanding after cutting, 136–137

  upcycling inspiration, 138–139

Bottles Uncorked, 139

Bradbury, Helen, 16

Brown, Lindsay, 16

brushes, paint

  applying sealants with, 79–81

  general discussion, 58–60

burlap coffee bean bag planters, 16

buyer persona, creating, 254

C

cabinets

  card file cabinet upcycle, 172–176

  geode, 12–13

  repurposed IKEA, 12

About the Author

Judy Rom turns trash to treasure, and so can you! On Earth Day 2012, Judy co-founded the upcycling website, Upcycle That (www.upcyclethat.com). Her mission was to galvanize a global movement, encouraging as many people as possible to upcycle! Over the past 10 years, Judy has created upcycling projects in the United States, Canada, South Africa, United Kingdom, Europe, and Asia and has inspired more than 3 million people to upcycle.

Judy currently runs Upcycle That from Vancouver, Canada, but her favorite thing about upcycling is how universal it is. No matter where you live, or how much money you have, you too can be an upcycler!

Judy authored *Upcycling Furniture & Home Decor for Dummies* to make upcycling accessible and fun. Get ready to reimagine the world, one furniture piece at a time!

Dedication

This book is for the treasure hunters — those who see potential in the old and discarded. Thank you for choosing to see beauty and for bringing it to life with your creativity and passion!

Acknowledgments

I am eternally appreciative of my wonderful parents, Marion and Stephen Rom, who stoked my creative fire from an early age. Thank you for supporting the authentic expression of who I am.

So much love to my Granny Dor, who showed me that character and value only increase over time. Thank you for the infinite amount of support and succulent clippings that you bestowed on me. I will forever treasure the time we had together in Cape Town.

Acknowledging my Grandpa Harry, from whom I am convinced my penchant for upcycling comes. I could still feel your presence in your workshop years after you had passed. Thank you for planting trees in the garden and for establishing the stable foundation from which our family thrived.

So much appreciation for my beautiful friends who love and encourage me. I am really blessed to have you all. A special thank you to my friend Bart Taylor at ReFind in Vancouver for being my supportive ally in upcycling throughout the years.

A big shout out to Jacques Karsten for recognizing the vision and potential of upcycling. Thank you for being the catalyst for the original Upcycle That website, and for pushing me to pursue my passions.

To everyone at the Dummies team — Charlotte Kughen, Kristie Pyles, Karen Davis, Mohammed Zafar Ali, and Kelly Henthorne. I am so thankful for the energy and care that you put into this project. A very special thank you to Dummies Senior Editor Jennifer Yee for finding me at the perfectly aligned moment and for stewarding this book. It truly means the world.

Publisher's Acknowledgments

Acquisitions Editor: Jennifer Yee

Project Editor: Charlotte Kughen

Copy Editor: Karen Davis

Technical Editor: Kelly Henthorne

Production Editor: Mohammed Zafar Ali

Cover Image: © Judy Rom, Champion of Upcycling at UpcycleThat.com

Leverage the power

Dummies is the global leader in the reference category and one of the most trusted and highly regarded brands in the world. No longer just focused on books, customers now have access to the dummies content they need in the format they want. Together we'll craft a solution that engages your customers, stands out from the competition, and helps you meet your goals.

Advertising & Sponsorships

Connect with an engaged audience on a powerful multimedia site, and position your message alongside expert how-to content. Dummies.com is a one-stop shop for free, online information and know-how curated by a team of experts.

- Targeted ads
- Video
- Email Marketing
- Microsites
- Sweepstakes sponsorship

20 MILLION PAGE VIEWS EVERY SINGLE MONTH

15 MILLION UNIQUE VISITORS PER MONTH

43% OF ALL VISITORS ACCESS THE SITE VIA THEIR MOBILE DEVICES

700,000 NEWSLETTER SUBSCRIPTIONS TO THE INBOXES OF

300,000 UNIQUE INDIVIDUALS EVERY WEEK

# of dummies

Custom Publishing

Reach a global audience in any language by creating a solution that will differentiate you from competitors, amplify your message, and encourage customers to make a buying decision.

- Apps
- Books
- eBooks
- Video
- Audio
- Webinars

Brand Licensing & Content

Leverage the strength of the world's most popular reference brand to reach new audiences and channels of distribution.

For more information, visit **dummies.com/biz**

PERSONAL ENRICHMENT

Staying Sharp
9781119187790
USA $26.00
CAN $31.99
UK £19.99

Facebook
Carolyn Abram
9781119179030
USA $21.99
CAN $25.99
UK £16.99

Guitar
9781119293354
USA $24.99
CAN $29.99
UK £17.99

Investing
Eric Tyson, MBA
9781119293347
USA $22.99
CAN $27.99
UK £16.99

Beekeeping
9781119310068
USA $22.99
CAN $27.99
UK £16.99

Digital Photography
Julie Adair King
9781119235606
USA $24.99
CAN $29.99
UK £17.99

Meditation
Stephan Bodian
9781119251163
USA $24.99
CAN $29.99
UK £17.99

Pregnancy
9781119235491
USA $26.99
CAN $31.99
UK £19.99

Samsung Galaxy S7
Bill Hughes
9781119279952
USA $24.99
CAN $29.99
UK £17.99

iPhone
Edward C. Baig
Bob "Dr. Mac" LeVitus
9781119283133
USA $24.99
CAN $29.99
UK £17.99

Crocheting
Karen Manthey
Susan Brittain
9781119287117
USA $24.99
CAN $29.99
UK £16.99

Nutrition
Carol Ann Rinzler
9781119130246
USA $22.99
CAN $27.99
UK £16.99

PROFESSIONAL DEVELOPMENT

Windows 10
Andy Rathbone
9781119311041
USA $24.99
CAN $29.99
UK £17.99

AutoCAD
Bill Fane
9781119255796
USA $39.99
CAN $47.99
UK £27.99

Excel 2016
Greg Harvey, PhD
9781119293439
USA $26.99
CAN $31.99
UK £19.99

QuickBooks 2017
Stephen L. Nelson, MBA, CPA, Aid to Taxation
9781119281467
USA $26.99
CAN $31.99
UK £19.99

macOS Sierra
Bob "Dr. Mac" LeVitus
9781119280651
USA $29.99
CAN $35.99
UK £21.99

LinkedIn
Joel Elad, MBA's
9781119251132
USA $24.99
CAN $29.99
UK £17.99

Windows 10
Woody Leonhard
9781119310563
USA $34.00
CAN $41.99
UK £24.99

SharePoint 2016
Rosemarie Withee
Ken Withee
9781119181705
USA $29.99
CAN $35.99
UK £21.99

Fundamental Analysis
Matt Krantz
9781119263593
USA $26.99
CAN $31.99
UK £19.99

Networking
Doug Lowe
9781119257769
USA $29.99
CAN $35.99
UK £21.99

Office 2016
Wallace Wang
9781119293477
USA $26.99
CAN $31.99
UK £19.99

Office 365
Rosemarie Withee
Ken Withee
Jennifer Reed
9781119265313
USA $24.99
CAN $29.99
UK £17.99

Salesforce.com
Liz Kao
Jon Paz
9781119239314
USA $29.99
CAN $35.99
UK £21.99

Coding
Nikhil Abraham
9781119293323
USA $29.99
CAN $35.99
UK £21.99

dummies®
A Wiley Brand

Learning Made Easy

ACADEMIC

9781119293576
USA $19.99
CAN $23.99
UK £15.99

9781119293637
USA $19.99
CAN $23.99
UK £15.99

9781119293491
USA $19.99
CAN $23.99
UK £15.99

9781119293460
USA $19.99
CAN $23.99
UK £15.99

9781119293590
USA $19.99
CAN $23.99
UK £15.99

9781119215844
USA $26.99
CAN $31.99
UK £19.99

9781119293378
USA $22.99
CAN $27.99
UK £16.99

9781119293521
USA $19.99
CAN $23.99
UK £15.99

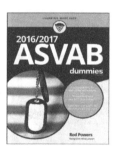

9781119239178
USA $18.99
CAN $22.99
UK £14.99

9781119263883
USA $26.99
CAN $31.99
UK £19.99

Available Everywhere Books Are Sold

dummies.com

Small books for big imaginations

9781119177173
USA $9.99
CAN $9.99
UK £8.99

9781119177272
USA $9.99
CAN $9.99
UK £8.99

9781119177241
USA $9.99
CAN $9.99
UK £8.99

9781119177210
USA $9.99
CAN $9.99
UK £8.99

9781119262657
USA $9.99
CAN $9.99
UK £6.99

9781119291336
USA $9.99
CAN $9.99
UK £6.99

9781119233527
USA $9.99
CAN $9.99
UK £6.99

9781119291220
USA $9.99
CAN $9.99
UK £6.99

9781119177302
USA $9.99
CAN $9.99
UK £8.99

Unleash Their Creativity

dummies.com